tion

Wie

RETHINK
WORK

FINDING & KEEPING
THE RIGHT TALENT

ERIC TERMUENDE

BARLOW BOOKS
fine books for enterprising authors

Library and Archives Canada Cataloguing in Publication data available upon request.

ISBN 978-1-988025-12-4 (print)

Printed in Canada

TO ORDER:
In Canada
   Georgetown Publications
   34 Armstrong Avenue, Georgetown, ON L7G 4R9

Publisher: Sarah Scott
Project manager: Zoja Popovic
Managing editor at large: Tracy Bordian
Cover design: Soapbox Design
Interior design: Kyle Gell Design
Page layout: Kyle Gell Design
Copy editing: Eleanor Gasparik
Publicity: Debby de Groot

For more information, visit **www.barlowbooks.com**

Barlow Book Publishing Inc.
96 Elm Avenue, Toronto, ON
Canada M4W 1P2

**BARLOW
BOOKS**

*For the two people who have always
supported me in ways I'll never fully understand
or be able to appreciate enough*

Mom and Dad, thank you

contents

Introduction

The need to re-humanize work is
stronger now than it has ever been,
and it is only getting stronger.

Whenever I step onto a stage to give a talk, I am nearly always the youngest in the room—by a long shot. I am twenty-four, and my clients and fellow-panelists are usually much older than me. They are managers of major companies or are sitting at the executive table, and they've been in those positions for quite some time. Each has far more work experience than I have garnered in the two years since I graduated from university. Yet, when we meet, these voices of experience usually ask me the same questions: Why are so many people my age quitting jobs? Why is this next generation so hard to work with?

Managers and executives are worried about a new and disruptive problem plaguing many North American companies these days: high turnover. Specifically, the high turnover of new employees, who come from the biggest age group in the workforce today. These are the young people under the age of thirty-five who companies recruit and train in hopes of building a powerful workforce.

It frequently doesn't work out that way. Instead of contributing to performance and profits, the employees my age often run for the door.

People age twenty-five to thirty-four stay on the job for a median three years. The U.S. Bureau of Labor Statistics tells us that is three times less than the median tenure of workers age sixty to sixty-four. It is a huge problem for employers.

Consider the cost of bringing in a new hire. There is the money spent recruiting new people, and then training them for the job. It takes time, especially in a small organization, to get the new hire up to speed, and in the interim, other employees or the employer have to fill in. The cost is huge, as a 2012 review by the Center for American Progress discovered. The average cost of taking on a new employee in a position earning less than $75,000 per year is twenty percent of the salary—or $15,000. It adds up.

Consider a thousand-member workforce with one-third of them under the age of thirty-five. Say one-third of those people leave every three years. High turnover is costing that company over $1.6 million per year. But if your organization is anything like the ones I talk to, the cost can be much, much higher. As one frustrated employer told me: it's like watching a Toyota putter into the garage—you transform it into a sleek Ferrari, and then it races out the door.

What's happening?

Consider this experience of a political science grad in her twenties—let's call her Helen—who took a job at a big bank in Kitchener-Waterloo. Helen got six months of on-the-job training in computer and filing systems, the basic financial concepts, and how to "engage" with clients. She also spent four months, at bank expense, getting the certification to sell some investment products to clients.

Ten months after starting work, Helen attended a daylong training program on how to market products to the bank's clients. She asked the bank's trainers: How do the bank's products differ from those of the competitors, and how have they been improved in recent months? They shut her down: she didn't need to know. "I simply needed to key in the client's information into the system, and the computer would dictate to me how to package and market the most appropriate product to the client. There was limited opportunity for critical thinking."

When Helen decided to leave, the bank offered her a promotion; she said no. "It wasn't the salary or seniority that really pushed me to leave," she said. "It was the monotony of the work combined with the fact that finance was not my passion."

Consider the cost to the bank of losing this promising young employee: Six months of training, plus four months of bank-paid certification. It all evaporated when she left the corporate behemoth. Finance wasn't even her passion, so why did the bank hire her in the first place?

Now, before we jump to say that this is Helen's fault and that she should have expected this experience in the profession she chose, remember this: there was no way for her to know what the experience of this job would be like. Helen was blindly going into a career she didn't understand. Was this her fault?

Partly: she didn't know what questions to ask; but also, the bank didn't tell her. The compounding effect is a problem that is not going to go away. In fact, it will get worse—unless we change the way we talk about work and what it means.

High turnover is a symptom of a dysfunctional relationship between companies and employees, and most companies still don't know what to do about it. Sure, they install a ping-pong table and offer up single-cup coffee and peanut-butter-and-jelly sandwiches for late-night work, but the young employees still leave for other jobs. And employers, like a jilted middle-aged husband, don't understand what happened.

This is what's happening.

There is a massive communication gap between job hunters and the companies looking for employees. Job hunters, many of whom belong to the biggest age group in the workforce (Millenials), are applying for jobs, but they have no idea what the workday at their prospective employer will be like. They don't know what the values of the organization are; they can't see anything on the job posting describing what work will be like. Meanwhile, employers are all but crossing their fingers and hoping for the best when they hire someone. By the way, this is not an issue of whether or not the employee has the skills or can learn them. They usually do—or they can learn them quickly. The problem is a mismatch between employee and employer on the things that really count: how you work, who you work with, and why you turn up every morning to do the job.

When an employee is unhappy, there are plenty of alternatives to check out on the internet. After a boring day at work, it is easy to scroll our social feeds and see more attractive workplaces. The competing employers may not be painting a true picture of their workplace, but they sure can make it look tempting—tempting enough for a less-than-happy employee to head for the door hoping and praying for something better.

Are employees asking for too much when they want to have jobs with a purpose, and jobs where they actually enjoy the people around them? Many older employers might say yes, they're being entitled brats. But surveys are telling us that this is the way it is today—and not just for the so-called Millennials. (Depending on the source, a Millennial could be anyone born from the late 1970s to the year 2000 and beyond.) At a time when we carry our smartphones with us everywhere, the line between work and home is getting thinner every day. This has enormous implications for work. Before the arrival of digital technology, we might have been able to work at a tobacco company, and then ignore our employer's activities on the weekend as we comforted our mother-in-law while she waged a losing battle against lung cancer. But today, that's not so easy, especially when anyone can see in an instant what we do on the job. We carry our work into our outside-of-work lives, and our lives outside of work into our work. We don't have jobs anymore; we have work-lives, lives that are integrated with work.

This digital revolution is redefining what work means at a far deeper level than most employers may appreciate. As most employers already know, it has changed how, where, and when we do our work. Some companies have adapted to this new digital reality with perks like rafting trips with the CEO, or workplaces that give you the choice between a monk-like meditative pod and a dining room table crammed with fellow travellers.

But we need a deeper shift.

We need to rethink work.

This does not mean that we have to change *what* we do. It does mean that to keep new hires, of any age, companies need to clearly define *how* people do their work, *who* they work with, and *why*. What comprises the life and experiences of those employees? Do they have the tools to do the best job possible, or is the employer still trying to control their Twitter feed? What kind of people work there? Is an introverted "numbers" person being plunked into a wide-open room of jovial salesmen who spend every night at the bar and then recount their exploits, in minute detail, the next morning? What is the purpose of the work being done? Does it make any sense for a member of the Green Party who cycles to work to take that accounting job at a car company or an oil company? Why, for that matter, did that poli-sci grad who knows how to ask good questions end up at a bank, which clearly wanted her to stick to the script?

Both sides need to be clear and honest in answering these questions. There is no point in faking it. New employees will figure it out on day one, and they will eat up the company training budget before informing the employer, perhaps a week before that big presentation, that they have found a new job. Companies need to be realistic about the kind of working life they are offering employees and what the experience at work is. They do not necessarily have to change; they just need to be authentic about the particular working culture that defines their firm.

There is no cookie-cutter solution, either. As I contend in this book: there isn't just one best culture. Every company has its own distinct working culture, and I believe the distinct working culture could even be one of the key things that differentiates a company from its competitors.

No matter what the company does, though, the culture must be about human beings. Workplaces of the future will address a basic human need that is currently unmet in many workplaces today. Those of us who have grown up in a digital world feel more and more isolated. We are accustomed to texting instead of talking with our neighbours—even when the neighbour is one desk away in a high-rise office. But the proverbial tide is turning. You can see the beginnings of a new trend in the CrossFit craze (described as "a fitness program that combines a wide variety of functional movements into a timed or scored workout"). People are tired of being alone. We want to work together, alongside other human beings. We crave old-fashioned human interaction. When work and outside-of-work life mingle, as they do today, we expect to be treated as whole human beings, not as a set of skills that are being rented from nine-to-five. So this is what the workplace of the future should focus on: belonging, community.

Companies that understand this will find ways to restore the human interaction as they recruit and train new employees. In this book, you'll read about how to connect to new employees in a way that will win their loyalty. It will be worth it—and not just to stop the waste of high turnover. If employees sense that they are at the core of a company's mission, and if they are connected to that mission, they will help the company increase productivity and its overall performance. Rethinking work, in other words, is not only the right thing to do for employees but also the way workforces of the future will need to be if they want to be successful.

The following pages do not describe how to cater to the next generation of workers. In fact, this book is not about Millennials, Generation Z (seen as those born from 1995 to 2010, depending on the source), or any other age group. It is about the changes that need to take place in the workplace for everyone's benefit, regardless of generation.

Rethinking work is vital for the future of any organization. Without it, employers will continue to see unhappy employees-of-a-certain-age stoke poor on-the-job morale until they quit. Companies will continue to waste millions of dollars on training employees who leave after soaking up the company-paid knowledge. Most of all, organizations that stick with the traditional ways of recruiting and managing their workforce will lose ground to the ones that rethink work and create a distinct culture that gives their people power and direction to achieve great things together.

I firmly believe that we can reverse the trend when it comes to poor tenure in the workplace. I know that workplace satisfaction can increase. If we make the workplace human again, and put people first, work as we know it will be work as we knew it, and we can create communities that grow, thrive, and, actually *work* well together.

1

Bigger than Work

No longer is work transactional.
It is now a stronger indicator than
ever before of who we are.

The workplace of the future is going to be a far different place because of the amazing power of technology that in many cases will let us work anywhere and anytime we want. In some places, this is already the case. We see the visible impact of technology everywhere throughout the day as those around us check up on news from friends, colleagues, and the world. It is so common a sight now that it is easy to forget that Facebook only launched in February 2004, with Twitter following two years later.

This new technology, powered by exponential improvements in digital components, is fuelling a revolution in the workplace. Technology has far-reaching implications that are still not fully understood, either by companies or by job seekers. It reminds me of what people thought about cars in the early twentieth century. Back then, they called the new inventions horseless buggies, as if the only thing to change would be horses going out to pasture. No one at the outset could predict that cars would reshape the physical environment, create new industries and new suburbs, and even change the air we breathe. (And this is just the beginning. Just wait until the Internet of Things disrupts the marketplace. With this development, where objects can connect with each other and send and receive data, it is projected that by 2020, an estimated 50 billion devices, or 6.58 per person, will be connected. In 2015, it was about half that.)

The Vanishing Line between Work and Home

The ability to work anywhere and anytime means we are importing work into our personal lives. Think of what it means to take a call on a Saturday afternoon from a colleague at the mining company where you work—as you are watching your seven-year-old son play his soccer game, or as you are perusing the movie listings to decide what you want to see that night. The colleague is pestering you to supply some crucial information—by Monday morning—about a mining deal your employer is negotiating in South America. You have read the disturbing story on your Twitter feed about how your employer, the mining company, took advantage of aboriginals living on the property of the dig site. How do you feel about that? In Canada, you volunteer to help improve the educational prospects of the First Nations kids in your community. You wonder: Does it make sense to be working for a company that undercuts the hopes and dreams of Aboriginal peoples thousands of miles away? And there you go, you just missed your son's goal as you frantically scrolled and swiped, with a bead of sweat forming on your forehead.

Now, I'm not suggesting you *had* to take that call. But the ability to do so in ways unavailable to you ten or fifteen years ago, and the reminder of what you do at work, means that your work life is mingling with your outside-of-work life. In fact, the line between personal life and corporate life is getting thinner every day. When we import work into our personal lives, it creates new expectations of what we do and how we behave at work. We expect the things we value at home, in our personal lives, will align with the things our employer values.

We Are the Work We Do

As work permeates our outside-of-work lives, we are increasingly defined by the work we do. Work has become a strong identifier of who we are and how we think of ourselves. (Think back to the last time you had a conversation with someone you had never met before. How long did it take you to ask what kind of work they did? It affects how you will relate to them. If you meet a thirty-four-year-old woman at a party who says she's a neurology resident, you are likely to have a different kind of conversation with her than you would with a surfing instructor or a bookkeeper of the same age.)

That is just fine if we like the work we do and how we do it. If we know there will be forty-eight-hour deadlines and weekend calls when we take the job, we will accept the situation and rise to the challenge.

If we don't like our job and how we do it, those expectations create an uncomfortable disconnect between the work we do and who we are. Chances are, we won't stay in that job for long.

Think How, Who, Why

To stop this waste of talent—and the loss of happiness and fulfillment—we need to think differently about work. Again, this does not mean we will be doing different things at work. We will still see accountants pouring over the books, lawyers puzzling over contracts, and sales people thinking about what their target market really wants and needs. That won't change. What will change is how we do our work, who we choose to do it with, and why. In other words, the purpose of the work we do, and the results of that work, must be clear.

As the work we do becomes a bigger part of who we are, it means that "work" needs to be bigger than work. In other words, what we do has to be connected to something bigger than just punching in and punching out: it has to represent who we are. It has to be connected to who we are twenty-four hours a day, as well as what we want to achieve and how we want to contribute.

Seeking Matching Values

According to Forbes, employees increasingly want to work at a company whose values match their own. A 2012 survey by Net Impact showed that fifty-eight percent of respondents would take a pay cut in order to work for an organization "with values like my own."

This is not just a question of getting a job that offers flexibility to pick up a youngster from school at 3 p.m. or take off on a Friday afternoon for a long bike ride. It is about aligning the values of the organization and the employees as well as the real on-the-job experiences that support those values.

From an individual perspective, our values are going to be what keeps us in the job. These feelings, of course, are what we feel from the experiences we have. We might, for example, treasure the feeling of passion. To get that feeling, we have to do things that make us feel passionate.

Values one might have are:

- to learn something new
- to be respectfully challenged
- to respectfully challenge others
- to build a sense of trust with others

Experiences that might make these values hold true are:

- travelling
- meeting new people
- connecting with a thought leader
- getting constructive feedback
- getting a seat at the table

For example, a junior salesman might say he values collaboration with peers, continuous learning, growth, flexibility, and freedom. Those are his values, but to make them real, he needs to have experiences on the job that contribute to rather than undercut those values. So what happens to him on the job? He works in teams with peers to help a retailer improve sales of tires. He gets weekly feedback, so he learns on the job. The client is happy: the team enabled a ten percent increase in sales. The salesman's need for flexibility and freedom is satisfied too. During the 120-day project, he only stayed at work past 5 p.m. on eight days. After finishing work on the project, he even went to Thailand with his girlfriend.

In this case, the on-the-job experiences delivered. You can be sure that salesman will be productive and will stick to the job. He might even help the company attract other like-valued people with similar skills, and help to create strong and productive communities in the company. This, I might add, is not just about catering to a new generation of workers to put a smile on their faces. When companies place the right people in the right jobs, the employees will be happier and will do a better job of serving customers and other stakeholders. Happy customers tend to stay with a company, and recommend the company to others too.

Finding Mismatched Values

Obviously, it doesn't always work out that way. The typical job description today does not describe the job, and job seekers both young and old are not asking the right questions. It leads to a disconnect between the company and the employee, between work and outside-of-work life. When an employee is working in an organization with a mission that does not resonate with his values, or when the way of working makes no sense to him, he probably will not do a great job. Both employer and employee lose. But now, we simply do not have the information to understand whether or not there is a true match. The description of the job is generally nothing more than a skills-and-requirements checklist.

A classic example of this disconnect occurred at one major bank in Canada. It hired numerous tellers in the usual way, just for skills. The bank did not tell the new hires what it would be like to work there, or why they might want to. As a result, the tellers stayed for only eight to twelve months(!). They knew how to do the job: the skills were easy to acquire. But they left because the recruiters did not describe what a day in their future life was going to look and feel like. If the bank were to outline a day on the job, and describe the people who did that kind of work, they might be in a better position to find employees who liked—and, therefore, stayed in—that work environment.

Here is another example from a former reporter at the *Montreal Gazette*. She was a go-getter who prided herself on delivering scoops and ideas for in-depth stories. She valued independence and freedom to deliver the best stories she could to the newspaper audience. When the newspaper added a Sunday edition in the early 1990s, every reporter had to work every second Sunday, even though that often meant missing a crucial weekday event. The inherent message of the new schedule was clear: no matter what you've accomplished, or how big the story you're exploring, you are a shift worker; you don't have independence, or freedom. It did not take long before a lot of the high performers, including my friend, left the paper. To be clear, though, this person is *not* a Millennial, and no more entitled than the next person. The environment was not well articulated, and it simply was not a good fit. All of this could have been mitigated with better proactive communication about culture and experience. In other words, an actual description of the job.

• • •

Portable technology is making it a lot harder to draw the line between who we are at work and in outside-of-work life. If the company's values undercut our own values, we may ask some hard questions about what we are doing, and why there is a disconnect between what we say to a colleague on our cellphone at 4 p.m. on Saturday and what we do in our life twenty minutes later. If you want to consider an alternative, technology makes it all too easy to find another job, seemingly more appealing, by Monday morning.

If we want to end the disconnect between our work and outside-of-work lives that technology can so vividly highlight, we need to drastically change the way we think about work. Keep in mind, though, that this is a positive shift. If the work we do is an extension of who we are, work won't have the same negative connotation it has now for many people.

Values and Experiences Matter More than Skills

It boils down to a simple proposition: when it comes to hiring—or getting hired—for fit, values and experiences on the job count more than skills. These are the things that are going to differentiate us from one another and build amazing places to work.

When Hiring for a Job

For employers, this means that instead of looking for people with only the right skills for the job, look for those who share the things your organization values, the feelings you treasure, and the experiences that cause you to feel that way. Then, if you are aligned, you can make sure they have the skills.

This is a big shift for most companies that are hiring today. They typically post notices with very specific requirements for a given job. They might insist, for example, on five years' experience in a senior business analyst position. There is little or no talk about the values of the people actually working in the organization, how they like to work, what their work means to them, and how work is connected to and enables the life they live. The focus is on skills, which are largely transferrable and often not industry specific.

You might think that makes sense. Yet this approach—looking for the skill set that fits the job—is not working as well as an approach that puts people first. According to a Future Workplace "Multiple Generations @ Work" survey, ninety-one percent of "Millennials" expect to stay on the job for less than three years. I can't really blame them (or anyone for that matter) for leaving, when the emphasis on skills alone is greater than the desire to truly discover and align the "why" of both the individual and company.

It is even worse in the big Wall Street or Bay Street banks. According to a LinkedIn analysis for *The Wall Street Journal*, analysts and associates who left their positions at a dozen investment banks in 2015 stayed an average of seventeen months, compared with a twenty-six-month average for those departing the same positions a decade earlier. Back in 1995, the average tenure was thirty months.

Many people are leaving jobs—just not because they lack the skills. In fact, they have the skills—that's why they got the jobs. They are leaving because after a few months in the actual workplace, they realized that life there was not what they thought it would be. As *The Wall Street Journal* reported, Wall Street investment banks are now facing the departure of young employees who are not satisfied with what the news organization described as the delayed gratification on the job. Resenting the drudgery and the lack of opportunity to learn new things in the early years, they are leaving. This early—and unanticipated—exodus is causing a real problem for some of the big banks that are counting on young people to make up for the forced departure of more expensive senior executives. However, the banks are not recognizing that the experiences and the values in the job did not align with the young employees' own values and how they wanted to work.

Recently, we hear a lot about work–life balance, and the ability to get work done at home, in a coffee shop, or, of course, at work. The ability to work flexibly is a big factor in choosing careers as well. We can now start to think about the lives we want to live and not just about the jobs we will perform from nine-to-five in the office. Many companies, though, have still not caught up and put the right policies in place to allow people to be the best they can be both within work hours, and outside. Failing to recognize people's lifestyles and to provide an opportunity for remote and flexible work, when possible, is certainly contributing to a large talent gap in the workplace.

To close the talent gap, companies should hire *first* for values and experiences. Then, once they have identified candidates who share their real values, they should make sure the person has the necessary skills—or can acquire them quickly. The non-starter should not be the letter grade or the .3 difference in the individual's GPA when there are *so* many people with the same skill as the next person applying. This is not a one-way street, though: the values of the company and the people within it should be well known to the employee as well. This is the difference between hiring people, and hiring people who stay.

The cost of getting it wrong is very high. Consider, for a moment, the cost to Telus of hiring Joe Natale as CEO to succeed Darren Entwistle. Natale, the company's Toronto-based chief commercial officer, had all the skills for the job, but he made it clear he wanted to stay in Toronto instead of moving to Vancouver, where Telus's head office was based. That seemed fine at the time; this is a communications company after all. But it did not take long before the company realized you needed the CEO to be at head office, in Vancouver. The result, as reported in *The Globe and Mail*, was this: Telus had to pay $24.1 million to bring back Entwistle and honour its commitments to outgoing Natale.

Ouch.

When Hunting for a Job

What is true for companies that are hiring is true for individuals who are job hunting. Typically, people looking for jobs acquire the skills for the jobs they think they want—and run up thousands of dollars in student debt doing it. Then they scour the postings on sites like monster.ca, LinkedIn, and so on to find the job that fits. The companies paint an attractive picture of a workplace where you can be "innovative" and "creative." Then the new employees get to work, only to find that in real life the companies live by the rules and punish failure. They cannot afford to be innovative or creative. After a few months, and thousands of dollars of company training, those employees leave.

Because work is bigger than skills.

It has to be.

Here is a typical example: One of my friends spent over a year of training and a few thousand dollars to be able to work as a veterinary technician.

She wanted to work with animals, in a part-time position, in a meaningful way. But as she was completing her first practicum, she found that the job had a very high level of responsibility and that it would require years of full-time employment to become confident and proficient enough to do it on a part-time basis. The job did not fit with her life.

She and I talked over the phone, and I realized that the idea of rethinking work—who we are and what we can get from our work other than a pay cheque—certainly is not specific to my generation. My friend is fifty-one, and she was asking the same questions that people thirty years younger are asking. We talked about the kind of workplace she would like to be in. Was it one where she worked with people often or rarely? In the office or remotely? Did she want a lot of feedback or not? Structure in her day or very little to none? Did she want to be creative or do something that didn't challenge her much? How did she want to report on the work she did? How did she want to be appreciated? How much did she have to earn to keep a roof over her head? What days of the week were available for work, and which were off-limits? As we worked through the non-starters and must-haves, we started to create a profile of the job, what it needed to look like to best suit her. In other words, we reverse-engineered the job search.

Next I told her to go through the whole process again with her husband. This was not because she needed "approval" or an "opinion" from him—it had nothing to do with him. Rather, this was because, from my experience, we can often tell ourselves things that we want to hear and not necessarily be true to ourselves. If we can have someone we love and trust guide us along the path of honest self-discovery, then what we put on the page will be who we really are and what really makes us happy. And that ultimately leads us closer to a job that will allow us to go home happy.

At this point, my friend and I had not talked much about the skills she had, which ranged from graphic design to event planning, bookkeeping, and being a trained veterinary technician. Once we defined the environment where she would excel and the skills she already had, looked at results-based as opposed to time-based expectations, we both realized that she should focus on a handful of jobs that might be a good fit. We then looked at positions that offered the feelings she was looking for and the experience she craved, all while being flexible and working remotely. Even though she was thousands of miles away, I could sense the relief and joy at the other end of the line. It felt amazing. The daunting world of work, something that offered tens of thousands of choices, was reduced to a mere fraction of what it was only an hour before we had talked. The weight that was lifted off her shoulders was significant. There were fewer choices, but for the right reasons.

• • •

In brief, portable technology is erasing the line between work and outside-of-work life, and it is causing us to rethink what work means to us. The message is:

- Employees are looking for work where the company values the same things they do. They want to have experiences at work that generate the feelings that they treasure.
- Employees want work that serves a purpose, work that makes them happy and fulfilled.

- The right job is not just about skills, either for the employee or for the company. It is about matching people and organizations who value the same things.

Work, in other words, is bigger than work.

2

The Real Joy of Work

It matters not what we do,
but how, who with, and why.

When we rethink work, let me suggest something that may seem preposterous: the things we do don't matter.

Let me explain. In the corporate working world, we all might be hammering on the keys for, say, thirty percent of the day, talking on the phone for another thirty percent, sitting in meetings for thirty percent, and getting from A to B for about ten percent. If we are doing vastly different jobs, but doing the same activities (especially in the corporate world), then perhaps the act of what we do doesn't matter as much. What counts, as far as our happiness and fulfillment at work is concerned, is how we do it, who we do it with, and why we do it.

Still, how can what we do not matter? We might be doctors, musicians, journalists, corporate lawyers, or bond traders. We live for our jobs. We love going to work every single day. How can anyone say that what we do doesn't matter?

What We *Actually* Do

Let's look at it a little more closely. Say I am a journalist at a big city newspaper. I cover provincial politics. Going over what I do during the day, we would have to admit that some of it is boring, or downright humiliating, like waiting in a media scrum to try to make a Cabinet minister say something that will create a page-one headline. So why do I like it? I like being in on the game of power, of having a front-row seat, of being able to potentially influence the decisions of powerful people. I like the status that comes with being a political reporter. It sure helps me navigate my way through a cocktail party.

In other words, I like the feeling, the reward of being a political reporter. I might even like that more than the actual work that I do on a day-to-day basis.

Or say I am a corporate lawyer. I tell everyone I love my job. But do I really like it when the client calls to complain about my $600-an-hour bill, or when I have to file reports detailing billable hours every day of my workweek? Perhaps not. I may like structuring a deal so that people can get together and make a project happen, but that is an admirable skill that can be deployed in many kinds of work, not just corporate law. I probably do like the pay, though. It is a reward, albeit a delayed one.

Or say I am a sales representative. I spend my days studying the market and my prospects. What do they want? How can I relieve their pain, or make life easier and more profitable? How will I get to know them, win their trust, and finally make the sale? I relish the feeling of winning when I make the sale. Does it make a difference whether I am selling a home, insurance, or pharmaceuticals? It doesn't.

So I suggest that it doesn't matter what we do, as long as we are connected to why we do it, and how it makes us feel. There will always be parts of the job we don't like, but if the overall feeling we get from the work we do is positive, perhaps this is most important. Perhaps this is what we need to identify early in order to find the necessary fit when attracting new people and creating great places to work.

A Meaningful Connection

Take the job of an accountant. Accountants have to pass some rigorous exams, but after they graduate, the experience they have on the job will depend on where they work. The life of a young accountant at one of the big firms will differ greatly from the accountant who goes to work at a non-profit, or in the movie business, or at a city golf course where perks include a round of golf four times a week. The young accountant in the big firm might say to himself: I'm enduring this so that I can gain the skills in valuation of publicly traded firms and then go on to a high-paying job at a financial services firm. The accountant at the non-profit, on the other hand, might say: Yes, I'm a numbers person, and I'm doing this because I want to improve the use of renewable energy and cut the smog in the big city. Meanwhile, the accountant at the film production company might say to herself: I want this beautiful film to be made, and it won't be made unless I can figure out the numbers and how we can get sufficient tax credits to stay solvent. Three accountants, three reasons why they go to work every day.

The point is that when we talk about our jobs, we rarely talk about what we actually do. How often do you hear the things a nurse *actually* does? Rather, we think about how we *feel* when we do our jobs. The nurse gets her satisfaction from helping people who are sick feel better, or at least feel less pain. The corporate lawyer likes the lifestyle she can afford. The political reporter likes the status of being an insider in a political game. The feeling they get from the work they do is more important than the work itself.

To be sure, some jobs give us immediate feedback. A singer on stage loves what she is doing in the moment. Other jobs offer a payoff much later, perhaps in the form of money that pays for a cottage by the lake and a golf club membership in town. Either way, what counts most is the feeling we get from our work, not necessarily the work itself.

Look at it in reverse. Let's say you are someone who loves being a doctor. You love helping people, but as a family doctor, you have to restrict each patient's time to fifteen minutes. That's not why you became a doctor. No wonder you're unhappy. Or say you got the job of your dreams at a prominent law firm. You loved studying law because of the intellectual discipline of finding a way to frame events and make a powerful, effective argument on behalf of your client. But now you're stuck in a place where you have to record billable hours in ten-minute segments. It's relentless. Then just as you're about to make partner, you become pregnant. The breakfast meetings and all-nighters aren't so appealing anymore.

Using this book as an example, I'm not a great writer, nor do I like doing it very much. This is the fourth time I've (re)written these words, and even then, I had to get extensive help with each section. But what I get from an experience like this is the same as I'd get from being on a stage: I crave reaction from people. I want to know that the things I've said or written have the potential to shape someone's life in some way. Tell me I'm wrong, and why, and I learn from you. Tell me I'm right, and how it impacted your work and life, and I'm thrilled for you (with an ear-to-ear smile on my face if you share your experience in a review on Amazon—win-win!) When writing a book, I have to wait a while, but the return is great.

The feeling we get from what we do is what counts, and we can get that feeling from more than one job. Take, for example, a former Olympic athlete I interviewed in early 2016. Like many athletes, he's highly competitive. He has spent a lifetime mastering his sport, field hockey. In fact, he made it to the Canadian Olympic team. He has a tremendous work ethic and team-building skills.

When he talked about his training, I could hear the passion and excitement in his voice. He did not talk about the fine points of running down the field and nailing the ball into the opponent's net. What he talked about was how he continually felt himself getting better. He spoke with passion about the feeling of mastery and getting closer and closer to his goal of an Olympic medal. Interestingly, this was also true of other athletes I interviewed. They loved the feeling they got while doing their sport—the wind in their hair, the companionship of their teammates, and the inching ever closer to their goal.

What he loved the most was the feeling of growing and improving, and the mastery of his sport.

Once his sporting life was over and he switched to the world of traditional work, he looked for employment that would deliver the same feelings that he got when competing as an athlete. When he talked to the right recruiter, and asked the right questions about a team environment, growth, development, and mastery, the recruiter ultimately found the right job for him. The difference was that he did not look for a job based on skills and education alone; he found one that *fit* who he was and the feeling he was looking for. This, of course, is best for both the employee and employer.

Feeling Passionate

How we feel about our work is crucial. I was in the audience at a conference in California in spring 2016 where bestselling author Martin Ford, author of *The Rise of the Robots: Technology and the Threat of a Jobless Future*, talked about how robots were going to replace humans in many jobs. He painted a scary picture: "Artificial intelligence is going to get smarter and automate jobs."

But one thing robots cannot do yet is feel, and feeling counts for a lot. If we enjoy what we are doing at work, customers will keep coming in because that passion is contagious. We won't leave that job anytime soon. If we are sulking at work, or cynical and resigned, customers and clients will feel that too, and they will take their business elsewhere.

That real-life passion means a lot. Take Tony Robbins. He has millions of followers and sells out shows across the country. He has the ability to move people to tears. Almost everything Tony does, though, is recorded. Why would I spend a few hundred dollars to see him speak when I could just watch him from home? Same goes with sports. Why go to Staples Center to see the Los Angeles Kings when I could watch from a comfy couch in my living room with a much, much cheaper beer? Because I want to feel the energy and passion from Tony and from the players. It is contagious and it creates an unmatched experience. I only get it by being there.

All of this might seem obvious. Yet, very few people look for jobs that can deliver the feeling that they want, and employers certainly are not telling the stories that make people ask the right questions. Job seekers are looking for either the brand name so they can make their friends and family proud or the job that pays the best. They are not thinking about their happiness while doing something that occupies more of their day than anything else (yes, even sleep): work!

I think one of the worst pieces of advice widely given is that people should try to find and follow their passion. Though always well intended, it promotes finding that "thing" that is always better than what we have. That the grass is always greener and we can always be happier. Instead, I think we should try to find the things that make us feel passionate. If we can do that, then we can look at hundreds, if not thousands, of careers and jobs.

Not *What* We Do

Finding joy at work comes through the how, who with, and why.

How

How we do our job is crucial. There is no denying the influence of modern technology, but beyond that, there are a multitude of ways to work.

For example, we can work at home, any time of day; we can work in the office, with scheduled or flexible hours. Some people relish the idea of working alone all day—others need to collaborate in-person with other people. Some like to take orders and execute them—some need creative space to work out problems on their own.

How work is accomplished is a crucial part of the company culture, but we do not talk about it enough. It should be clear to anyone who is applying to work at that company. Turning the above examples into questions can help reveal this when job hunting: Can employees work from home, setting their own hours, or must they work fixed days and hours in the company office? Will I work on my own or in a team? Will I be expected to follow pre-set directions precisely or can I develop my own approach? (Or turn the examples into interviewer questions: Would you ideally like to work from home, setting your own hours, or to work in the office, Monday to Friday, 8 to 4? and so on.) The key issue is that how work is done should be accurately and clearly addressed in job interviews. If questions are not asked or answers not sought—by either party at the interview table— the working style may not be an ideal fit for the job hunter or the company looking to hire.

Who

Who we work with is an integral consideration in determining how long we stay on the job.

In numerous interviews over the past years, I often ask people what they like most about their jobs. Most often, the first responses are that they like the people, or that the culture is great, again usually because of the people. Are they people you want to have a beer with after work? Are they people who make you feel productive and creative? Or do they undercut your confidence, or make you feel it is only about getting ahead, whether or not the project is a success?

When we talk about who we work with, we often start with the job title, but then very quickly get to talking about what we like or do not like about them. When these emotions are discussed early in the conversation, it is much easier to get a broader sense of the environment of the workplace, and a better sense of who is working there and what the culture is. As we will see in the next chapter, the people, and how they work together or against each other, form the crucial cultural backdrop for any job. But that cultural profile tends to be invisible.

Why

The feeling of fulfillment and happiness at work is largely connected to a clear purpose of why we're doing what we're doing, especially in those organizations that are attracting people based on fit and with a clear mission. So for starters when job hunting, we need to understand the purpose of the company. Is it aligned with the change that we want to make in the world around us? In my own research, I have found that non-profits have an easier time than for-profit companies in recruiting because they make their vision, mission, and desired impact abundantly clear. In some cases, they could not offer the same salary, but they could still find the right people because the cause was so compelling and the fit was so clear. People join together, and join organizations, because they share a vision of the lives they want to live.

Not every organization can come up with a noble purpose, but we should still be able to say why we have chosen to work there. In many cases, we are there because it's a great place to work. When I ask people what they like most about their job, they usually say the people—they are friends and they like working together. This is what connects us to something bigger than just the tasks we do. The work community is a reflection of who we think we are.

3

Work in an Optimized Culture

*A universal best culture
does not exist. Optimizing culture
is much more effective.*

Finding the right match between an individual and a job is not easy. As we have seen, it is not just about finding the right skill set for the job. We have to make sure that the individual and the company workplace are aligned when it comes to the things we value, the way we work, who we do it with, and why we do what we do. In today's business language, we are talking about a cultural fit—something I think is not well understood.

The Right Culture, Not the Best Culture

We know cultural fit is important: surveys tell us that young people are looking for the "right cultural fit" in the job. But what does cultural fit really mean? In my opinion, a "fit" means that the individual working in the organization is aligned with the other people, the environment, and the outcome of the work that is being done. It is not something that everyone can agree on, and has nothing to do with age, gender, ethnicity, and so on. It means that there is no pressure to perform and be someone they are not. It means being the best version of who they are and knowing that is okay, and exactly what the organization they are working for needs. We'll talk more about this later.

But is this definition, or a slight variation of it, universally accepted? I don't think so. Let's take business magazines, for example. These publications love lists, so they give us lists of the "best companies" to work for. *Fortune* magazine, for example, rated the top 100 companies to work for, which in 2016 included Google (a perennial Millennial favourite), Baptist Health South Florida, and Wegmans Food Markets, Inc.

What does that tell us? Not much. In fact, if I am looking for a job with a "people and cultural fit," this top-100 list—covering industries such as tech, health, and groceries, just to name a few—tells me nothing other than the people already working there are happy. In fact, these fine companies have nothing in common, except that people apparently like working there. But who are those people? People who like working for a grocery chain are likely very different from the people who get picked to work at Google in terms of what they like to do for work.

Asking people who have never worked in a company to participate in a survey does not help. When asked to rate the top companies to work for, Millennials typically answer Google, Apple, and Facebook. But why? Most Millennials have never worked there, and never will, but they are being asked to rate those companies having experienced nothing about them other than using their products and perhaps reading about them. It is like people being asked to rate their favourite place to travel having never been there, or their favourite music never having heard it. To me, this is ludicrous—almost as ludicrous as the fact that we try to rate the best companies to work for, or the best cultures, universally.

When companies say on their websites that they are one of the "top 25 companies in America" to work for, because of their "people and culture," it probably means they know how to hire the right people. But it means nothing from a job seeker's perspective. It does not say whether the applicant looking for the job will be the right person who will stay for five years and contribute to the well-being of the company, or whether he will stay five months and leave because the real-life culture of the place did not fit his expectations. It also does not speak to who that person is, how they are aligned with the company's values, and what life they like to live outside of work. All of these things matter.

In other words, if we are looking for a cultural fit, the brand name of the company does not matter much. The real issue is whether the individual looking for a job is the right person, in terms of cultural fit, for the specific workplace that needs help.

It is not about finding the best culture. The first step is about finding the *right* culture.

The Postcard Effect

Companies often fail to paint an accurate picture. Take the job posting I found on monster.ca for a sales position. The company said it is looking for someone who is "committed to ensuring that our environment is barrier-free to all persons, employees and clients alike, as we believe in equal opportunity. In the spirit of this philosophy, we are committed to providing reasonable accommodations to all applicants with disabilities in the interview and assessment process."

Huh?

These empty words do not say anything about what it would be like to do the job or about the people who work there. These job postings are designed to sound appealing, like the postcards people used to mail home from Europe in the twentieth century—"Having a wonderful time in Paris this summer"—when in reality they got food poisoning at an overpriced restaurant, the weather was muggy, and the tiny hotel room didn't have running water for a day of the stay.

At best, these company descriptions of "the culture" represent one percent of real life on the job. It is natural to talk about the best parts of the job, though. We employees do it too when we post tidbits of our lives on social media. Take a look at your Facebook account or Twitter feed, and you are bound to see friends and acquaintances crowing about the great lives they say they are living—the exotic trips to Phuket; the smart conferences in Manhattan, followed by drinks and dinner at an ultra-cool place on the Lower East Side. The typical thirty-year-old reads this and wonders what he's doing in a 500-square-foot condo in midtown Toronto, a few grimy subway stops away from his $43,000-a-year job. No wonder he looks elsewhere; the postcards from the company websites look awfully appealing, until he gets there. Let me be clear, though, this is not just a Millennial problem. This is a conversation about the accessibility of information and the lack of depth in the information we see.

I call it the postcard effect: when we see—or present—only a sliver of what the experience actually is. And it isn't limited to just travel. We see it in dating profiles and job descriptions as well. Perhaps on our trip to Phuket there was a flat tire on the chicken bus we rode into the city. When we got there, it was pouring rain and the hostel we stayed in was smelly and slept sixteen people to a room. Yet the postcard we sent Mom and Dad only described the sunny beaches with the classic long-tail boat on the shore.

Defining Workplace Culture

To me, culture is the interaction between an employee and the environment he or she works in. The environment would include anything from the aesthetics and atmosphere to the people and tools required to do the job. Culture is how people talk about their jobs both inside and outside of work hours. It is about both the experience they have and how they feel about it. A good culture, then, would be one where there is a positive relationship between the environment and the employees; a negative one would be the opposite.

A workplace that has established a good culture would mean that the people within the space do the best work they can do because they *want* to, not because they feel they have to. In a place with good culture, all the tools are present to do the best work possible, and the people that are present generally share the same values and desire the same experiences. When people are in a workplace they enjoy, the conversation about the brand, space, leadership, and environment is positive both inside and outside of the workplace, and people have a sense of belonging.

In contrast, a poor culture is one where there is tension and friction, where people do not feel positively connected to the workplace and people within it. Conversation about the company is generally negative, and people work because they *have* to, not because they want to be the best they can be. There is a lot of staring at the clock, increased distraction, and decreased productivity.

An Optimized Culture

Attending the 2016 Milken Institute Global Conference in Beverly Hills as a speaker, I had the pleasure of hearing Harvard professor Dr. Bob Kegan's presentation. Co-writer of the recently published *An Everyone Culture: Becoming a Deliberately Developmental Organization*, he talked at length about how a great culture is one where people feel neither driven to the bone nor on vacation. In an optimized culture people are able to just "be." They do their work well because not only do they solve problems but also problems solve them. By this, I mean that they can learn from the problems and get better at their job while still getting the job done. In these workplaces, people learn and grow together without feeling that they have to constantly perform.

What he said made total sense to me. Imagine how much more capacity we would have if we did not feel that we had to perform and please all the time. Where we did not have to worry if we were doing too much or too little and were just able to be our best because being our best just made sense. This, to me, is the optimized culture and one we should all strive for. Imagine a world where people did their best work because they wanted to, because they were connected to the purpose and people. Some might say this is not possible, but the hopeless optimist in me (someone who is experiencing this for himself) believes that if we can find the right fit one person at a time, this can actually happen.

The idea of culture may sound very subjective and, of course, it is. An environment that may be a good fit for one person may be a terrible fit for another. Culture does not highlight or focus on sex, age, race, or experience; it includes all people. To suggest that a "Millennial" culture can be established is incorrect since Millennials vary as much as anyone else.

There is no such thing, then, as a best culture. It may be the best for one person working there, but it may be unproductive and simply not feel right for another.

The key comes down to having an *optimized* culture, one that is the best fit for the people within the company. You cannot externally benchmark it or compare it to other companies: the people in company X may really not enjoy the culture established in company Y. Most importantly, the culture has to be understood by everyone—from the CEO to the people on the ground floor.

Reality Check

Some companies are trying to hire for cultural fit by telling applicants about their carefully crafted mission, vision, and values statements. But what does it mean to "stand firm for what's right," or to "raise the bar," or to "have commitment to each other"? What do these words mean? Do the people in the company understand what they mean and put these values into practice every day of their working lives? If not, they are mere empty words.

The postcard version of reality on the job does not help achieve the right cultural fit, for either the companies or the individuals working in them. Yet these postcards are filling the digital space and confusing both companies and individuals. For the job applicant, it presents an illusion of great choice. We see an unrelenting stream of happy pictures from companies looking for recruits. It is not real. It is not us. But we would never know it from the images in the digital world.

We live in an artificial world that has created the illusion of unlimited choice. Yet it does not make the people I know happy. It makes us anxious, because we always think that someone else, somewhere else, has a far more exciting and glamorous life than we do. After all, we can see the vivid images on our phones and laptops. The grass is always greener, right?

There is a big gap between the artificial images of work, as seen on company websites and our favourite social media, and real life on the job. It is very disappointing. Sure, we might get hired and take the job. But when we get there, and see what work, as the company defines it, really means, we don't say long. Why should we? There is always another place to go.

Thinking about this gap between illusion and real life in the job, it seemed to me that neither employees nor companies should settle for a work experience that fails to bring out the best in the employees and to make them productive, long-term contributors to the well-being of the organization. I thought a dose of authenticity and radical transparency might help.

What if a company were transparent about what it actually is like to work there?

Consider this. Many major theme parks now post wait times. Having been to Six Flags and Disneyland, seeing those two-hour lineups is obviously less than ideal. But what do I do? I wait, and contribute like everyone else to making the line a whopping two hours long. And generally speaking, none of us complains. We knew how long the line was going to be, and we chose to wait in it.

Studies show that if we are told how long it will take to get to the front of the line, we are more willing to wait in it. In some cases, the wait times posted are often ten percent longer than the expected actual time. As a result, if we are standing, for example, in a grocery store line and we get to pay in nine minutes instead of the posted ten minutes, we feel like we have won a minute of our day back.

Taking that same approach, what if a company told the real story of the experience it offers, with the people we would share it with, and from the point of view of employees who work there? In their own actual, unfiltered words?

Think, too, of the employee. Perhaps, think of you. If we could get *you* to say what you liked (and didn't like) about the job, this could create a real picture of what life was like at the organization, and why people like you would want to work where you work, and even work with you. Employees could have meaningful influence in the hiring decision by helping to attract those job seekers who would be the best fit.

The idea sparked a whole new venture.

The Cultural Diagnostic Tool

I set out with my colleagues at Gen Y Inc. (now The DRYVER Group) to create a cultural assessment tool to find out what employees themselves really thought about working in an organization. We wanted to know what they felt about their work, and why.

Our Cultural Diagnostic Tool was designed to help articulate the values and experiences of people working in each organization. By understanding what people loved about their job, we could not only create content for a recruiting document that would bring people to the organization based on "fit" as opposed to the draw of brand or salary but also help companies solve problems like succession planning, leadership training, inclusion, communication improvements, and more within their workforce. Here was a chance for employees to speak up and say what they thought, without fear of reprisal. If we could empower people to make their voices heard in a confidential and anonymous way, we could help drive change and align culture. This exercise in transparency and discovery uncovers truth about the experience at work that can be both showcased and improved upon.

We ask employees questions, initially in the form of an online survey, about things such as how they perceive mentorship, leadership development, contributions, fulfillment, collaboration, and so on. Then we approach employees in person and ask them for stories (that remain anonymous) that could paint an even better picture regarding their feelings about working at the organization. We might ask them to tell stories about how they stayed overtime to get the job done, or what their job enabled them to do in terms of travel, teamwork, and conflict management.

The questions, of course, depend on the nature of the particular business.

After gathering the information, both the online responses and the stories, we analyze it. For example, in the case of a fast-growing resources company in Western Canada, we could tell young mothers in their thirties liked working there because they had control over their lives. Older Aboriginal men felt immense pride. Men in their twenties joined the company for risk and adventure. It was interesting to see how different their perceptions were, and it helped the company hire people in all three demographic groups.

This deep dive into the culture has helped companies solve the problem of why, after absorbing a lot of expensive company training, so many employees are leaving. At one company that was experiencing a retention problem, the employees said they did not feel appreciated for their efforts. This was news to the executives, and the CEO took quick action to commend good efforts in a personal way. Two months later, we could see that the employees were happier, more engaged, and doing better work as a result. Or take the technology company that had taken the trouble to write mission and vision statements. The trouble was that none of the employees knew what they meant. Then there was the old-school warehouse office, uncomfortable and noisy. It was an unhappy, tense place. The employees told us that people were not talking to each other and that no clear direction was evident to them. After receiving our report and plan on how to move forward, the executives saw the problem and acted accordingly. They set up monthly meetings to talk about the company vision, and what it meant in real life. The office was renovated. The result, of course, was that employees felt more empowered after having their voices heard, and this built a greater sense of engagement. They were more aware of what they were contributing and how it was being used.

Understanding the Existing Culture

When going into companies, we are often asked to create culture, as though it does not exist. In truth, the culture is there, and it cannot be created or destroyed. It can, however, be aligned and improved. The employees know what it is, and they tell us. The problem is that real life, as experienced by the employees, may not be the same as what the higher-ups think it is. Our goal is to identify where the alignment could be, and help shape the direction of the company to ensure that each person feels a stronger sense of belonging and more aligned to the values of the company.

Understanding culture is crucial when it comes to attracting the right talent. But there are many pitfalls. Comparing and contrasting company cultures is a waste of time and money. To suggest that because a pool table in one office is used and enjoyed by employees, putting one in another office will cause those employees to be happier does not make sense. Therefore, we use our tool to watch a company culture evolve, year after year. We have found this the best way to gauge whether the company is making progress in creating an *optimized* environment for its employees. Another might be the idea of remote work, or even working flexible hours. Much of shift-work today can't be completed at any other time or location. This doesn't mean the culture is any better or worse, and the story that is being told must include why people are there and love their jobs if the company is trying to bring on more people looking for a similar experience.

Early on, we found that culture could vary significantly within a single company, from department to department, especially in larger organizations. In each place, the values and experiences differed, and for good reason. In companies with hundreds of employees, an accounting department is very likely to have a completely different vibe than the sales group, or the marketing department. As a result, we looked to segment the data and articulate what the employees in each department loved about their jobs. This way, the company could share different stories that were relevant to and tailored to reflect the culture of the accounting team, the marketing team, and so on.

At the end of the day, culture is how people interact with their work and talk about it both during and after hours. It is everything about the people in our companies, what they value, and what they want to experience. Understanding the culture reveals whether people have the ability to do their best work because they want to and not because they feel they have to.

Why It Works

The success of the Cultural Diagnostic Tool does not depend on asking exactly the right questions every time. What matters is asking questions that people have not been asked before. We empower people to have their voices heard—for many, this was the first time, and it changed the way they communicated and worked with each other. Important to note, too, is the anonymity of the analysis and the trust we gain with employees before starting. Management does not see the data; we do not ask for names or email addresses, and are not able to filter the data to pinpoint who said what. The tool also shows whether the commands from the top of the company make it to the floor, where people are working. By asking questions, we can see what resonates with people and what doesn't. Rather than culture definition being a traditional top-down exercise, this empowers people at all levels to be involved in the process, and in the shaping of the company culture. It gives them a powerful way to contribute, and feel part of it all.

Benefits All Round

This is not a frivolous exercise—for either employees or companies.

We spend most of our day at work, so it is important to know how we feel about it. If the job does not feel right, there are plenty of other options. The Cultural Diagnostic Tool can help employees see their workplace, and their relationship to it, more clearly. And it offers them the opportunity to contribute toward creating an appealing place to work—not a postcard, but the real thing

Companies can learn what their employees actually think about the work environment. Where needed, the employer can improve or correct the situation and, thereby, maybe retain employees for longer. Furthermore, the stories employees share can help attract the next group of employees to the organization, people who already see themselves as a fit.

The greatest benefit is an optimized workplace that everyone who chooses to work there can love.

Let me tell you, making that happen is a hell of a feeling.

· 4 ·

The Fictitious Millennial

A Millennial is a false construct.
We are all simply people with different
values, skills, and experiences.

As mentioned earlier, depending on the source, Millennials are those born from the late 1970s to the year 2000. A Millennial could be a thirty-five-year-old chartered accountant, a twenty-eight-year-old rapper, or a twenty-four-year-old author, entrepreneur, and international speaker like myself.

What are we supposed to have in common? Well, almost all of us have "grown up digital," to use the words of Canadian technology guru Don Tapscott. We are the first generation to grow up with the Internet, cellphones, and social media, and many experts say it has shaped our minds, our values, our ways of being.

That may be so, but what does it mean? We are supposed to be addicted to our devices, uneasy about being alone, eager to share every moment of our lives. They say we are entitled, lazy, pleasure seeking, content to hang out in our parents' basement watching the latest on Netflix. We can't focus; we're distracted by silly things. We don't buy things. We just rip off musicians and filmmakers by downloading stuff for free. We don't respect authority, or the value of hard-earned experience on the job. We just want to skip to the top of the ladder as fast as possible with no regard for the time and effort it takes to get there in a reasonable manner. Sound familiar?

Have you ever heard this complaint? "The children now love luxury; they have bad manners, contempt for authority; they show disrespect for elders and love chatter in place of exercise. Children are now tyrants, not the servants of their households. They no longer rise when elders enter the room. They contradict their parents, chatter before company, gobble up dainties at the table, cross their legs, and tyrannize their teachers." Socrates wrote this over two thousand years ago.

Stereotypes Blind Us

The media like labels, and the lazy Millennial image suits them just fine. The problem is that the stereotypes distort the image of an entire age group.

Let's take, for example, the PwC report *Millennials and Financial Literacy: The Struggle with Personal Finance*. Millennials in United States, the report tells us, have "inadequate financial knowledge." Only twenty-four percent of them demonstrate basic financial knowledge. That sounds bad, until you ask the question: Are people in their twenties today any less knowledgeable about finance than their parents were at that age? Are they any less knowledgeable than older Americans, who typically spend more time thinking about the cost of a fridge than they do about the in and out fees of a mutual fund they are buying from their financial advisor? In fact, the report gives a tantalizing hint: Millennials show "better" knowledge on mortgages—a topic they intently study. They are not as good as other age groups on inflation—no surprise, since inflation is at a historic low. They are not as good on "risk diversification"—again, not a surprise when you consider they would not have a lot of money to invest in the market as, sensibly, they are repaying student debt.

You get the idea. The report is a prime example of a survey (in this case, of 4,400 Millennials) that is conducted to achieve one key goal: confirm the client's point of view.

May I respectfully suggest that the year of my birth does not define me, or anyone else. This may come as a surprise to communications, media, marketing, polling, consulting, and other such companies who think that age and use of technology is defining my generation, just as the Second World War and Woodstock defined two of the generations before me.

In fact, I do not think you can define any generation. Think of the Woodstock generation. Some of them became community activists, yoga instructors, and quilters; others went to Bay Street and concocted the financial shenanigans that nearly drove us into another recession. Most of them never even went to Woodstock.

It is easy to generalize, though. You can say something about us and you will probably be right, because it will be true for some people—but not everyone. Sure, there are lots of young people living in their parents' basement to save money while they are looking for jobs, or starting new ones. (No wonder when the average student debt in Canada is $25,000, which is substantially higher than the student debt of their parents' generation.) To say they are irresponsible—for example, more irresponsible than the bankers who brought us the 2008 financial disaster—is simply incorrect.

Google has an interesting view on this. Its human resources department collects and analyzes a wide range of data about its huge workforce. The so-called Millennials, as an age group, are not very different from anyone else, Google's HR chief Lazslo Bock told the *New York Times* earlier this year: "We measure this sort of thing closely, and if you look at what their underlying needs and aspirations are, there's no difference at all between this new generation of workers and my generation and my father's generation." He went on to say: "Every single human being wants the same thing in the workplace—we want to be treated with respect, we want to have a sense of meaning and agency and impact, and we want our boss to just leave us alone so we can get our work done."

It is true that my generation were early and enthusiastic adopters of digital technology. Sure, we taught our parents how to "log on" to their computers. We showed them what the Internet was, and how to go to a website. We introduced them to Facebook and Twitter. But now, they are in. People of all ages have been transformed by the digital world. It has changed the social norms for *everyone*, not just Millennials. Emails, texts, Twitter comments, Facebook posts—all have become a fact of social life. In fact, the fastest growing cohort on Facebook is grandmothers.

It is true that young people are worried about economic factors that did not press so hard on their parents—such as the high cost of housing, big student debt, and the chase for a job. These are important concerns, but they affect everyone, not just young people. Last I looked, houses in Vancouver are not priced higher for twenty-eight-year-olds than they are for forty-five-year-olds. Still there is no doubt that people my age are more affected by these economic trends than are fifty-year-olds. We are at the age when you look for your first job and buy a house.

But economic factors do not exclusively define who we are. Think of it this way: in the last couple of decades the stock market has inflated many portfolios. Does that describe who those investors are? Do they think of themselves as a lucky stock market winner? Probably not (even if they are glad it happened). They are a proud parent, a great teacher, or maybe a helpful professional who resolves difficult problems. So why do people insist on thinking about my generation in terms of the economic conditions we grow up in?

My generation, comprised of nearly eighty million North Americans (conservatively, depending on the year range we choose as defining a Millennial), is the most ethnically diverse generation in American history. We are a big group, with some commonalities among the individuals, and also with other generations. For example, I am twenty-four years old. I value deep debate. I enjoy constant learning and a little risk. I like to be challenged. I enjoy the pressure of having to deliver on time. And by the way, I can't figure out which remote turns on the TV, and I call my brother when I have to do anything more complicated than opening a Word document. I might have a lot in common with someone my age—and with someone in her fifties. These qualities are not age specific.

Sure, there are trends and shifts in how people work in a digital world, but these trends are not unique to Millennials. For instance, Millennials like flexible hours, but so do forty-five-year-old mothers who want to hit the beach or work from home, and fifty-five-year-old men who want to be able to play golf on Friday afternoons and catch up on work over the weekend or in the evening. Plenty of people—not just Millennials—want to avoid the commute and instead work from home or from Starbucks.

The Internet is opening up spectacular opportunities. Even in a small city like Cranbrook, British Columbia, you can be as connected as you are in downtown Toronto. If you do not like your job, you can pack your bags and go somewhere that is more appealing. This is true for anyone, not just Millennials. Questions about work, such as why work eighteen hours a day in finance and work through major holidays, are not restricted to the young. Older people want fulfilling work that makes them happy, too. And now, with information as accessible as it is, we can all explore where the greener grass might be.

Seeing the Individual

I think it is time to drop the stereotypes behind the Millennial label. They are not real, or authentic. The articles on Millennials do not describe all people my age, nor do articles on other generations capture everything about them. And when companies put out well-meaning reports on Millennials that play off the stereotype, I just have to laugh—and I'm not the only one.

Why, for instance, do they define a generation in terms of a fifteen-year cohort? If you see the Millennials in terms of their use of technology, that fifteen-year definition does not make much sense. Technology is changing fast and delivering new life-changing services like Facebook at a dizzying rate. So why not shrink the span of a generation—to six years, or even six months?

In fact, bottom line: age does not matter. What matters are values—the things people care about.

So here's a novel idea: why don't we treat employees (and all people) as human beings? Maybe some of them have things in common, but those are probably not defined by their age. Some might be introverts who like to fiddle with numbers in a quiet office; others get their joy from connecting with people, exchanging stories, and moving step by step toward the big sale.

If we start treating people as individuals, not as members of a stereotyped generation, we may find that there is a better chance of recruiting the right person for a job. When reaching out to a customer who happens to be age thirty, we may find our pitch is more successful if we listen to him as an individual, instead of checking off the boxes of a corporate profile of his generation.

Companies that find ways to connect with employees, partners, and customers of my generation as individual people will be successful. Companies that think the way to learn about these people is through expensive surveys may find that the "real" people in that age group are deserting them.

5

A New Way to Recruit

*Telling stories is better than
listing requirements.*

Not too long ago, in my fifth year of university, I was doing all I could to get my first job. I had been a vice-president of a student club, had participated in extracurricular business case competitions, and had been elected vice-president–operations and finance for the Students' Union, an organization responsible for the fees and select services for twenty-five thousand students. All in, the Union had an $18-million annual budget, which I was ultimately responsible for. In addition to that, I was selected as one of five class ambassadors for the graduating class of 2014.

At that time, my goal was to be a consultant or business analyst for one of the big players. I was not too concerned about which industry, but coming from an oil and gas city in Canada, it was either a consulting firm or oil giant that would be my best bet. I sent out my resumé to about twenty-five different companies, and got one call back. True, my grades were less than stellar, but I thought that my on-campus experience would earn me more than one response.

That wasn't the case.

Job Hunting and the Robot Gatekeeper

I struck out in the traditional job hunt. It turned out that everything I wrote on my resumé did not matter. All that mattered was having a few keywords that would impress the robots that scan the incoming flood of resumés to see which ones make it to the short list. As everybody but me seemed to know, screening software, known as Applicant Tracking Systems, goes through submitted resumés to find matches with the job posting. Now you can go online and make sure your resumé has the words that count for your target job. It could be words describing so-called hard skills, like "metrics" and "customer-facing," or soft skill words like "dedicated" or "passion." Robots, it turns out, are making the first call on my generation's job prospects.

A generation ago, you might have seen a job posting on the university bulletin board, or on a trade newsletter. If you applied, you probably got an interview, and if it was a really juicy job, you might be competing against a dozen people. Today, a single choice job at a consulting or financial firm might attract thousands of resumés.

Google, for example, receives over two million applications each year from around the world. On average, 1 in 130 people will get a job. In other words, the odds of getting a job at Google are much worse than they are of getting into Harvard.

Demographic trends are driving this problem. According to research done by Ilona Dougherty, Statistics Canada says that the number of Canadians between the ages of eighteen and twenty-four in post-secondary university has doubled since 1980, even though the population of young people has declined three percent in that period. These university graduates are ambitious, driven by school and parent expectations to score that big job—the six-figure consulting or accounting job, for example. When they get it, parents are thrilled; their job is done. That is the Holy Grail of success, as it is being defined right now.

When it is time to hunt for a job, young university grads naturally rely on technology. It is easy to make a template resumé and cover letter that can be tweaked for each potential employer. By the end of the day, I can send these off to scores of companies in the hope that one will impress the robot screening the emails.

The screening systems were introduced to cut the cost of hiring new employees, which in 2012 averaged $3,479, according to human resources consulting firm Bersin & Associates. Big companies spend about seven percent of their external recruitment budgets on Applicant Tracking Systems, the firm said in a *Wall Street Journal* article.

I can't say I blame companies for resorting to robots when they are confronted by a tsunami of applications, but this process is a gigantic waste of time and money, for both job hunters and companies. Let's say George goes online and constructs a resumé that matches ninety-nine percent of the keywords demanded for a particular job. He gets in—to what, he doesn't know. All he knows is that he scored a job in a company with a famous and attractive brand, maybe even one of that year's twenty-five best workplaces in Canada. But he does not know the real stuff: What is it going to be like to work there? What kind of people is he going to work with? He never talked about that on the resumé, and the robot screening the resumés clearly did not care. Once he starts work, if he is not aligned with the company culture, he is headed for a massive letdown. That is when he starts hunting for a job all over again.

The Traditional Way to Post a Job

Companies that are hiring people contribute to the mismatch with job postings that focus on skills. Take a look at this typical job posting I found on a monster.ca search for an analyst position.

Financial Analyst (Business Analyst)
About the Job

Under the responsibility of the Finance Manager, the Financial Analyst will prepare reports for key decision-making, to include financial statements, and will analyze balance sheets, expenses and budget accounts. S/he will focus on variance and trend analysis, financial modeling, and prepare documents and presentations.

Responsibilities:

- Prepare annual budgets, quarterly projections and reconcile revenue recognition
- Assist the manager during month-end closure to ensure accurate and timely information
- Reconcile and analyze assigned balance sheet and income statement accounts and explain variances (trend and correlation)
- Provide timely, relevant and accurate reporting and analyze financial results, monitor variances, identify trends and explain significant or unusual fluctuations
- Prepare and analyze weekly, monthly, half-year and full-year reporting to ensure proper accounting procedures have been followed
- Identify and track revenue and expense trends

- Ensure accurate and timely invoicing and analysis
- Assist the Finance Manager in the preparation and maintenance of financial forecasts as well as annual budgets
- Ad-hoc financial analysis
- Perform other duties as assigned

Requirements:

- Bachelor's degree in finance, accounting or business; a combination of other education and experience will be considered
- CPA designation
- Two (2) years or more experience in accounting and finance
- Knowledge of:
  - Financial concepts and principles such as cash flow, balance sheet, cost of capital, depreciation, tax reporting, etc. (advanced level)
  - Oracle Hyperion Essbase, Smart View and Walker (advanced level)

Although this is a great skills and requirements description, this certainly *isn't* a job description. The job hunter does not gain any understanding of what the experience of the job would really be like. Nowhere does it say what the life of the people who work there is like, how they do what they do, and why they do it.

Scrap the Lists, Tell Your Stories

Traditional job postings are not the way to recruit the ideal candidate. Companies need to start looking for that small percentage of people who share their values. How?

We need to rethink the recruitment process so that companies have effective ways to find the people who share the company's values and way of doing things. The job description cannot be a list of buzzwords that are targeted at young people; it has to be much more. To create a good match, there has to be a clear understanding of what both the employer and the candidate value, and what kind of experiences will make those values real on the job. The idea of radical transparency and authenticity has to be at the forefront of every recruiting document.

What if companies tried something different? Instead of buzzwords and algorithm-beating phrases, companies might tell a story of the job and talk about the experience of the people who are working there. If the cultural description was clear, it would act as a filter for applicants. Interested people could list their skills and explain why they want to work for the company and help make its mission and vision come true. The resumé would then be a follow-up document and not an entry point. For sure, it would be more time-consuming to apply, but it would also be easier to identify the right fit. Think of the mutual win.

This takes more steps, but it would spare the company the cost of a wasteful interview process, plus the cost of training someone who leaves three years later.

A New Way to Post a Job

Let me give you two examples of what I mean by a job posting telling your company story.

The DRYVER Group

Here's how I would write the job posting for a business analyst at my company in Vancouver.

Example of someone we love in this position:

Eric Termuende [I'm a narcissistic Millennial so, of course, I'm going to use myself], a 24-year-old analyst who has been with us for two years. He lives in downtown Vancouver and walks to work. Usually he gets in around 7:30 a.m. and stays in the office until about 5 p.m. He works in a pod with three other people who are all extroverted, and tends to hang out with them both inside and outside of office hours. Eric spends a good part of his day on the computer and on the phone, but is often asked to meet with clients out of the office too. Last year he travelled to six countries, two of which were for work, and was able to maximize the efficiencies of two of our systems. Work for him is creative, but within the confines of our requirements, and often has to be taken home because of the high demand of the job. Eric worked 150 hours of overtime during the evenings and weekends last year, but because of our flexibility, was able to extend his work trips to include personal pursuits as a result.

Throughout the day, Eric collaborates with his team to solve high-profile problems. The work he does involves a lot of teamwork and collaboration, and he is often put in high-pressure situations where it is either sink or swim. Each day is different, and each day he learns something new.

Eric meets with his senior twice a week and was invited to two board meetings to be a "fly on the wall" to know what is happening, but not to have an equal voice as he doesn't have the experience or organizational knowledge to do so.

Eric likes to get outside as much as possible and lives an active lifestyle. Before work he will often be at the gym, and after he can likely be found doing something social outside with his peers. Eric shares these values with the pod he works in.

His favourite moment last year was being able to meet with the company president for an hour and have his ideas heard. Eric told us that the president called him after to thank him for his time, and that his ideas were very much appreciated and helped propel the company forward.

Does this sound like an experience you want? If yes, check out some of the skills and characteristics you need for the job.

Skills required:

- Proficiency in Microsoft Office
- Loves to build relationships
- Loves to connect people
- Is outgoing
- Takes calculated risks
- Is entrepreneurial
- Tells a good joke

Experience required:

- Bachelor degree
- Sales experience
- Has given a presentation
- Has been on a stage
- Has played an organized sport for more than 4 years

Company:

The DRYVER Group

This job description does not really talk about the day-to-day tasks, but what it does do is talk about the experience of one of the valued employees. It talks about what he values, what his day looks like, and what some of his experiences are. If this is something that a job seeker wants to experience, then proceeding to the skills and requirements would be a logical next step. Based on this description, though, someone who is introverted, wants to work by themselves, and desires a very flexible workday would not find this job a good fit.

This description talks about the environment the employee works in, what type of people he works with, and what he likes to do in his spare time. Sure there are sacrifices, but if an individual wants the job, sugar-coating the position and suggesting no over-time is required would not be doing the organization or the potential employee any favours. Hiding the true experience of the job isn't a mistake; it's just a costly delay—an employee will find it all out within the first two weeks of the job anyway. Be proud of the position being offered, tell the experience as it is, and attract an individual who would own the position, feel purpose in doing the work, and thrive in the company of the people around her.

Descriptions like these allow people to *feel* more and understand what the actual experience on the job might be like. By understanding the lifestyle someone is able to live as a result of the job, it is easier to identify what some of the non-starters are within the job, and how it might be a fit for people wanting not only a job but also an experience.

As a job seeker, if I wanted to work in the same company as Eric, I would think about my cover letter (or video resumé) describing how I am similar to Eric, and why I might be a good fit there. If I desire the same experiences and have the skills and/or education required to do the job, there should be no reason why it wouldn't go to me as opposed to someone else.

Bench

In Vancouver, Canada, there is a new accounting company that is exploding. Bench closed a $20-million investment round in May 2016 and is seeing massive growth. But what impresses me most about the company is that they make the life of bookkeeping look fun.

Pictured below is a screenshot from their website, https://bench.co/career. As you can see, the focus is on the people, not the task. Why? Because if people like who they work with and feel aligned with them, it isn't about the work itself: it is about the community created.

Angad
Accounting Team Lead

Daily meetings:
4–7

Most commonly used emoji:

I tried out just being myself and learned that people enjoy who I really am. I know when I walk through Bench's doors I am the same person as I am outside — that's why I like being here. As a team lead, I show up to work as who I really am and I make sure that my team and my colleagues get to do the same.

Apply to work with Angad

As I explored further, I thought Angad would be fun to work with, so I clicked for more.

Here is what I found:

We're a laid back group of people working hard on a tough problem. Bookkeeping is a universal point of pain for passionate entrepreneurs trying to pursue their dreams. They want to run their businesses, not do accounting, so we make that disappear. While the appeal of bookkeeping may seem lacking, we genuinely believe that solving fundamental business problems is super sexy. And so are you.

When you throw in with us you're not only joining a company that's changing the way business is done, you're joining at an inflection point. Bench is post Series B, capitalized by a team of Silicon Valley and New York investors. We're scaling fast and we're not slowing down anytime soon. In just a few short years, we've grown from four co-founders to over 200 Bench-mates. It's been quite the ride so far and we're looking for the brightest minds who love solving tough problems to join us on this incredible leg of our journey.

What's an Accounting Associate?

As an Accounting Associate, you'll be in the midst of the action, at the core of what we do. Bookkeeping is a universal point of pain for passionate entrepreneurs. They want to run their businesses, not do accounting, so we make that disappear. You'll not only be completing month-to-month books for our clients, you'll become an essential part of their entrepreneurial journey. Not to mention the positive, hardworking, genuine, and all-around awesome human beings you'll get the chance to work alongside.

What will you be doing?

- There's a lot to learn and a lot to do—straight up. Your first 2–3 weeks will be spent with our Learning & Development team in our self-directed training program to equip you with the tools and resources needed to become the know-all of bookkeeping

- Our clients rely on us for their bookkeeping needs. Whether that's completing bookkeeping trials for new clients, getting a backlog of books up-to-date, or doing month-to-month ongoing bookkeeping, you can expect to be number crunching on a daily basis

- You'll be given plenty of autonomy in your role while also participating in collaborative, team-based meetings and discussions
- There will be times where you'll branch out of your direct team to collaborate with other departments (Sales, Client Care) to fulfill the needs of our diverse clientele

What do you need?

- Preferably a post-secondary degree in business, science, or math. You don't need a background in accounting, but you believe in the bookkeeping work that you'll be doing and how it fits into the larger picture of why we do what we do
- Have a positive attitude and an appetite for learning and continuous development to thrive in our fast-paced environment
- Can roll with it. You can adapt to changes in processes, while at the same time asking questions and sharing your thoughts and ideas

Other details:

- This is a full-time position, because we want to spend lots of time with your wonderful self
- Our office is downtown and easily accessible via transit
- This position offers an annual salary based on experience
- We offer an extended benefits package that includes health, dental, vision, massage, and a Wellness Fund
- Best of all, you get to play fetch with our resident Wheaten Terrier, Zoe Deskennel

Sound like the role for you? Hit "apply" and let's get this thing started.

In my opinion, this is the *Mona Lisa* of job descriptions. There are mentions of transit, dogs, focus on attitude, change, autonomy, and more. Take it from Angad, it is a great place to work!

Recruiting Tips

How can you tell if a candidate is the right fit and shares the same values and ways of working? It is essential to get to know the individual and to have them get to know the company. The following are some ways to help that happen.

Be Yourself

It is important to be yourself, even if you are a company. Eager to find new recruits, it is all too easy to end up projecting an image that does not reflect real day-to-day life in your company and in the job.

Being yourself is especially significant when a lot of competitors offer the same kinds of services that you do. Be yourself when you are hiring and you will differentiate your company from the competition. Telling prospective employees how current staff work together, who they work with, and why they do what they do will help employers find and hire the right people, the ones who will stay long enough to make a real contribution to the company. That translates into a long-term plus for a business, its customers, and for differentiating the company's position in the marketplace.

Being yourself means not comparing yourself to other companies: a benchmarking exercise is a mistake. A credit union I know tried to benchmark their culture against a big bank. They wanted to know how their people compared to those in the bank, and how they could improve their operations to be more similar to that of the bank, which was much larger and had a much stronger bottom line. While this may seem like a good idea, bigger is not always better, and sometimes the smallness of a company is what makes it unique. Being yourself may mean recognizing that the intimate culture of your small company could be one of the drivers that makes the organization and the people within it a success.

Interview for Values as well as Skills

The interview process needs a rethink. Often, whoever does the interview—HR, a manager, or even a senior executive—ends up checking the CV, or the list of skills that are supposedly needed for the job. Or sometimes the interviewer just operates on instinct: the candidate looks the part, or comes with an impressive academic or work-history background, so he must be good, right? It is rarely enough.

Interview in the Place of Work

Many organizations do second or third, even fourth, interviews, but from my research, these interviews do not take place in the actual work settings. Frequently, a candidate is taken out to a fancy dinner or to meet the team in a setting that does not reflect who these people are at work. It might not be as glamorous to move these meetings to the work environment, but it will be more authentic and accurate. To get a better grasp on what the environment really looks and feels like, interviewing in the office and getting to know people more is important when making a decision that dictates how we spend the majority of our day.

Have the Candidate Interview an Employee

Another suggestion, and something I have done, is to provide the candidate with a set of questions to ask an existing employee about their experience in the position. It gives the candidate a unique way to explore if the job is going to be a good fit. Again, finding out early that it isn't saves a *lot* of time and money—even if it takes a little longer to find the right fit. Mitigating disaster is much better than having to react to it.

Here are some of the questions I have given people to ask existing employees:

- Do you have a family at home? How much time do you spend with them?
- How many hours do you *actually* work in a week?
- What do you do for fun?
- Do you hang out with people from work?
- What is feedback like in the office?
- Do you feel appreciated here? Why?
- What is your favourite part of the job?
- What is your least favourite part of the job?
- Why do you work here?
- What is one piece of advice you'd give me before taking this job?
- Where have you travelled in the last year?
- What have you created while at work?

By the end of this interview, the candidate will have a much better idea of what it is actually like to work in the organization, but also what life would look like, having heard from someone already in the position.

Reverse the Interview Roles

What about a *reverse* interview, one that gives the candidate a chance to interview the potential employer? It is a new idea, one that might surprise the candidate, so I often suggest to corporate clients that they give the person some questions to ask. The candidate's reaction—and if they springboard from those to questions to some of their own, and what those are—might also reveal insights into their fit with your organization.

Job Shadow for Fit-ness

By job shadowing, the candidate will actually be able to see how the workplace functions and what it would be like to work with the staff, should they get the job. This inexpensive exercise, though time intensive (perhaps even a week or two), saves money in the long term. This would, of course, happen later in the recruiting process—after initial interviews suggest the candidate is a fit for the job and the company, but before the final decision is made. The decision to work together has to be made by both the employee and the employer, and job shadowing can serve as a helpful last litmus test for both.

• • •

Does recruiting sound like a lot of work? It is. But companies have to see hiring as an investment in the future, not a cost. Hiring people is not a matter of filling a seat; it is about building an ecosystem. Putting people in a position that allows them to be their best because they want to be, and not because they feel under pressure to be, is far more effective.

If we are rethinking work, we must rethink recruiting. We are recruiting not just for a job but also for a way of life. We are no longer asking questions only about skills for the job; the experience at work is much bigger and all-inclusive than that. Instead, we are asking people if they want to be a part of our team, our tribe, our family.

The shift to make a working world that is a positive, empowering experience is happening now. By focusing on the individual as opposed to the generation, gender, or ethnicity, and by recruiting in a new way, we can start to create some very powerful workplaces where we can be our best with people we want to be with, and do things that we feel connected to.

6

The MVP Statement:
Mission, Vision, and *People*

If the company and employee are truly aligned, the values of the company are the values of the people.

Mission, vision, and values: It is the first thing I hear when the conversation turns to organizational culture. These are the drivers behind organizational success and are what keep the company on track. These are the words and accompanying statements that are framed and hung in the office lobby and proudly displayed in the boardroom.

All too often, though, they are boring platitudes, like this one: "To satisfy our customers' desires for personal entertainment and information through total customer satisfaction." Seth Godin (American thought-leader) unearthed this meaningless corporate jargon a few years ago when he challenged his followers to find the worst mission statements in the United States.

North American companies spend millions of dollars developing mission, vision, and value statements. They are supposed to be at the very core of the work we perform. So why is it that so many of these statements posted on the wall go unread, and mean very little? Why is it that so many employees either do not know their company's mission and vision statements or mutter disparaging comments when someone reads them out loud?

When it comes to recruiting, people should know what the mission and vision of the company is in the job interview. If I were against big pharma, then being placed in Pfizer probably would not be the best fit. Similarly, if I was ultra "green," then working in the oil patch is not something I could own, regardless of the skills I had and the job I was going to fill. That's not all, though. People need to crave the same emotions and have the same desires—the ones that are summarized in the company's statement on values.

The Role of Mission, Vision, and Values Statements

Isn't it time to rethink this essential part of working life?

The mission is supposed to be what the company is trying to do. Every single person in the company should know what it is, and how they are contributing to the goal. It is crucial. The mission keeps people together and ensures that they feel they belong in the workplace and are working as a team to move the needle forward. Without it, and without buy-in from all members of the company, an organization can falter because there is no clear direction. Employees will leave and the workplace will become increasingly fragmented.

Vision is supposed to be what will happen if the mission of the company comes true. For example, if the mission is to put a roof over the head of every homeless person in the city, then the vision is to have a city that is free of homelessness. If people can buy into the purpose of the company then the work to make the mission come true will be done more efficiently and effectively as each person will be hoping for the mission to come true.

Vision reveals the true purpose of a company; why it is doing things. Say there is a non-profit with a mission to provide clean drinking water to five thousand people. Their vision is to create a healthy community. That is pretty appealing. But imagine we are talking about an oil and gas company with a mission to become one of the top producers in the country. The vision then would be to fuel more cars, and provide more power to customers. This might not be as inspiring as the healthy-community vision. It is not surprising, then, that many companies struggle as they try to write their vision statement.

The values part of the statements trio can be the most problematic. Values are supposed to be what the company needs to hold true to in order for the mission to come true. Employees need to share those same values or they are not real, and not supported. This can be a challenge, even if the organization starts out with shared values from top to bottom. As a company grows and matures, the offerings and services change, as do the market and buyers, and even the people working there—and with that, the values may change.

All too often, the values statement ends up being empty or abstract words that no one understands or feels. For example, a telecom company in Canada listed some of their values as "integrity, loyalty, balance, and team player"—which does not really tell us much, does it? We cannot measure things like integrity or balance, and different people might interpret them different ways. A meaningless values statement can be harmful because it can invite cynicism among the employees—cynicism can be a virus that spreads quickly through the workforce, undermining joy, creativity, and productivity.

The Role of People in Making a Statement

If we want to stop the waste of high turnover and increase job satisfaction, we need to rethink these important statements. To be sure, the mission statement still needs to say what the company is doing, and the vision statement still needs to say why the company is doing it. But for the third defining driver, companies should focus on who is doing the work.

People, in other words, should be included in these essential statements. In fact, I think we should create MVP statements—mission, vision, and *people*. The P would describe the people in your company who make it work—as Mark Bowden would put it, what "tribe" they are part of—and would include who they are working with and how.

At the 2016 Canadian Internet Marketing Conference, we learned there are over 3,874 digital marketing agencies, all of which do many of the same things. Where they differ, though, is in the people who work in the companies, how they do their work, and why. Ultimately, it is the culture that varies and not so much the tasks themselves. People could be a key differentiator for each of these firms as they seek to hire the right employees.

Highlighting the people and the company culture will bring the mission, vision, and people statements to life and differentiate one organization from the next.

In early 2016, I met Giovanni Marsico, founder of the Archangel Academy. Within seconds of meeting him, I knew we would get along. The clarity he had around not only himself but also the values of his organization made it easy to converse with him and understand exactly who would be a good fit for him and for the Archangel community—not because of the skills these people had or the work they were doing, but *who* they were.

Through his work with the Academy, Giovanni aims to bring together young entrepreneurs and hugely successful older ones to figure out how they can make a fortune and make a difference at the same time. The vision is a grand one: to make the world a better place. But take a look at the website (www. archangelacademy2017.com): it is mostly about the people, the feelings, the experience of belonging to this incredible group. There is no hard sell to sign up for the Archangel Academy (you actually have to be invited). If you are referred by Giovanni or one of the team, they will send you an invite and ask that you apply for the Academy.

They are not selling anything, and they do not push what they do onto anyone. Instead, they build a tribe. Their message is: We think we share the same values and could benefit from each other. If you want this experience, we want you too.

To take this a step further, in a conversation with Giovanni, he said that he has so much trust in the people in the group now, that he isn't in on every call anymore, and he doesn't have to be at all of the meetings. That is what happens when everyone is aligned, believing in the same mission, vision, and values.

It is a great example of how people—real people who are customers or members of an organization—can reveal the tribe that is your organization. There are no abstract words on the walls. People themselves, and the expressions on their faces, tell the story in a far more convincing way.

The P in the MVP statement are critical. A company's brand, how it is perceived from within, and without, is the people who work there—who they are, what they like to do, how they work, and why—and their relationship to the company's products and services.

Let's return to the example of the oil and gas company I mentioned earlier. They might still have their mission to be one of the top producers in the country, and the vision could still be to fuel the cars that drive us to work and to heat our homes at night. That is what will happen on the outside if the mission comes true. But the people part of the MVP statement could say what the company does on the inside: employ X number of people, contribute X dollars to communities, and support X number of families. To know that the people are a part of the organization's success, are valued in its growth and development, are part of the long-term success of the company is surely something that will put smiles on the faces of the team.

Look at what Suncor Energy did after a disastrous fire wiped out part of Fort McMurray in northern Alberta in 2016. The company plane airlifted stranded pets out of town and back to their owners. The picture of a Golden Retriever on the plane seat said it all. This is a company that cares about people, and the pets they love. Not only is this a good thing for the community, it is also great for employees who support the oil and gas projects. It is a strong indicator of who the people of Suncor are, and not just another description of what they do.

When people are working together to achieve the same mission, when they are about the same things, it's magic. They work together as a community, and when the community becomes stronger, people feel more comfortable and they can produce great work.

• ● •

The new MVP statement I propose does not necessarily mean that the people in the company will do anything differently. It simply challenges how we tell the story of what we are doing and who we are doing it with. If we talk about people, and not just the delivery of products and services, then we have what I call the new PR: People Relations.

It always comes back to people.

7

Workplaces to Love

*Building communities, tribes, and
great places to work is the key to
retention and workplace satisfaction.*

Back in the day, before digital technology, offices were noisy places.

When we wanted to say something to a colleague, we would walk over to her office or cubicle and talk, or maybe shout. That was, of course, before technology entered the scene. Now we do not talk to one another like we used to; we text, email (five sentences max, I recently read), use Slack, Snapchat, or WhatsApp. Instead of sharing a story, we share a link. Instead of an around-the-table board meeting, we meet up in Google Hangouts. Meaningful communication in the office is at an all-time low.

Workplace as Lonely Place

Offices have gone quiet. Technology has dehuman-
ized the workplace, and from what I have seen in my
work, this is adding to anxiety on the job, a situation
that psychotherapist and business consultant Jona-
than Berent told *Forbes* magazine is "an epidemic"
and that the American Institute of Stress describes as
having "escalated progressively." Employees spend
increasingly more one-on-one time with their computer, trying to decipher the terse two-line messages
dropping (relentlessly, I might add) into their inbox.
In some offices, managers are not personally training
young people anymore. Human training has been
replaced by onboarding videos and tutorials. There
is little or no effort to introduce a newcomer to his
fellow workers. Now, one of the biggest complaints I
hear is that people *actually have to meet*. Crazy right?
They are upset that so much time was "wasted" when
the meeting could have easily been replaced by a
Skype call or virtual group chat.

We can be sitting by someone we love and care
about with all of our hearts and still be on a phone
looking for external validation and approval from
people we have not seen or heard from in years. We

can be in our offices, sitting a few feet away from someone, and barely make eye contact or talk to them for hours on end. Instead, we wait for our inbox to fill up, our phone to light up with a notification, and some sort of task to be assigned to us digitally. I think that this lack of human contact, this isolation, is causing anxiety in the workplace that has not been experienced before, and that people are doing all they can to feel a sense of belonging, a sense of reliability, and a sense of appreciation.

Technology is supposed to allow us to share, but we grow increasingly further apart from one another. Perhaps in a world that is more connected than ever before, we are *connecting* less and less. Compounding the problem is the way companies typically hire. When they hire for skills and not for values, it is hard to form a genuine community at work.

So, what is the point of being in an office if we do not interact with our boss or co-workers in person? If we are going to text instead of talk, why do we have to be at the office? A lot of people do not see the point, which is why we often see them hogging the couch at Starbucks only a few feet from a decent cappuccino, computer on their lap with their headphones in. Let's be clear, though: this isn't right or wrong, it just is.

It is a lonely way to work, though. Not surprisingly perhaps, some people camped out at Starbucks are now craving community. The honeymoon phase of flexibility and freedom to this degree is over. Many people want to work in a place where they can chat with the person at the next desk. They want to build relationships, friendships, community. They have found a way to do this in co-working spaces that are popping up all over the country. In these spaces, people are still free to come and go as they please, but they are working with people who like to work in the same way they do. That is why they will pay a relatively small amount for a desk space each month to use the shared bathrooms, boardrooms, and kitchen area. It is great for start-ups: members of the team can meet at the co-op space when they need to establish personal contact. But for people who are popping in instead of working at their company office, something is missing: you can't pop over to the couch under the window and discuss a problem face to face.

This is likely going to change.

Workplace as a Belonging Place

My bold prediction is that within the next ten years people will migrate back to the office where they can meet up with people in the same business. Sure, flexibility will still be encouraged, but if we love our workplace, and the people in it, why would we want to escape and work remotely? We wouldn't.

If people go back to the office, though, what kind of workplace will that be?

To love a workplace, will a ping-pong table be required? I think this is one of the biggest myths about the workplaces of the future that are supposed to suit my generation. The stereotypical image includes a beanbag chair and a ping-pong table, and maybe a keg. These are supposed to be the toys that will induce employees to stick around. I think they have it all wrong. That is not what it is about. Sure, these will be present in some workplaces, but a foosball table is not required in an office with good culture.

What we do need is a sense of belonging.

Being Your Best, Naturally

To gain insight into what the new generation of workers wants, take a look at the CrossFit culture. When you are at a CrossFit class, you are the best you can be, among peers and friends who are not only doing the same but are also holding us accountable while working with others on a clear goal for a limited amount of time. You're not performing, you're just doing. The writing on the walls (literally) promotes only the best, most positive work ethic, and the feeling we get walking into the room inspires us to be who we really are. These experiences are something we do with people who share the same values as we do and crave that sense of belonging, or fitting in.

Collaboration

It sounds a lot like the culture of the start-up entrepreneurs. These days, many start-up entrepreneurs do not work alone. They are collaborative—people organize in teams to get things done. They are personal. There is a sense of friendship and camaraderie. You can be innovative and creative, to be sure, but you get a lot of help from your friends. You do not have to worry about hierarchy or management. You just have to be the best version of yourself to get the job done.

Camaraderie

Both entrepreneurs and people who do CrossFit need camaraderie. It is a need for belonging that many members of all generations share. Now we can create a workplace to love if we hire the people who share our values and want to join the community. Workplaces to love will be communities of people who have conversations about things that include both work and life outside of it. When this happens, it will enhance the feeling of belonging for each person in the office. Then people will want to stay.

Tech-Free Space

Alhough we may have more "friends" online than ever before, I firmly believe that in many cases we are living in a time that is also more lonely. If we can create environments that bring back traditional communication and relationship building, I believe we can create workplaces that people will truly love. In that workplace of the future, we will move away from a dependency on phones and from distractions so that we can have more meaningful conversations with the people standing or sitting beside us. There is more noise in the world we live in now than in the past. Beyond distracting, it can be alienating.

To counter this, I think workplaces should have a tech-free space or times that people could opt to use when trying to be creative or collaborative. This space might have paper and pens, a whiteboard and markers, and a recycling bin. To be in this room, people have to either turn off their phones or leave them at their desk and come to the conversation with nothing more than an open mind and a set of ideas. This concept would make sense in a world that is becoming increasingly connected virtually and disconnected practically.

Jasky Singh, a director at K2 Audio Visual and Tech Entrepreneur, made this point in a recent piece he wrote in *Medium*. He was having a hard time being productive; the digital devices were too distracting. He finally found the solution on a plane trip overseas when both his flight entertainment and reading lamp were broken. He did the only thing he could think of: he started drafting emails and writing notes in Word. These were some of the most productive hours he had worked in a long time. There was no noise, no distraction, and nothing that was pulling him away from his work. Whether he liked it or not, he was stuck in his seat for several hours and could not move.

When he got home, he replicated what happened on the plane in his everyday practice. For two hours a day, Jasky turns everything off—Wi-Fi, cellphone— removes all distractions, gets into a hyper-productive state, and just focuses on pure work. On Twitter, he called this time *#flighttime*.

I think that if this practice could be incorporated into business on a large scale, then not only productivity but also workplace satisfaction would increase substantially. It would be even more interesting, though, if we could incorporate #flighttime as an opportunity for meaningful interactions with our co-workers—without the presence of technology. I think that if we could connect in a meaningful way and interact with people without any distractions, significant progress and benefit could occur on various fronts within an organization, and morale and inclusion would increase dramatically.

People and Culture Make the Workplace

There is no formula for creating a workplace that everyone will love. It depends on the people that are working there, and the environment they are in. If we can understand the dynamic of the people in our workplaces—how they like to interact, how they feel when they go home, and how they feel when they walk in the door in the morning—it will be much easier to maintain the culture we have created. In other words, the head office of Google might be great for the people who work there, but not for the people in an advertising company in Vancouver.

Choice and customization will be key features of the workplace of the future. We are living in a world where we can order pizza online and have 250 different combinations of toppings. We are living in a world where our cars and clothes can be customized infinitely. We are living in a world where we can choose any job, in numerous countries, and in any sector.

So why can't we customize the workplace and give each employee the tools to do the best work they can because they *want* to, not because they feel they have to?

Humans are not designed to sit at a desk for eight hours and be productive for all eight of them. In fact, according to a *Fast Company* article, there was a study done by "the Draugiem Group, a social networking company ... Using the time-tracking productivity app DeskTime, they conducted an experiment to see what habits set their most productive employees apart. What they found was that the 10% of employees with the highest productivity surprisingly didn't put in longer hours than anyone else. In fact, they didn't even work full eight-hour days. What they did do was take regular breaks. Specifically, they took 17-minute breaks for every 52 minutes of work."

Some workplaces have already put an end to the traditional eight-hour day at the desk. In Silicon Valley, many offices have a gym, bar, games room, nap room, collaborative lunch space, creation room, wifi-free space, and a way for everyone to do what they want to do, when they want to do it. This does not mean that everyone in each organization will want to do all of these things every day, nor do these items mean that the culture is great. In fact, there may be some people who never use the bar or the ping-pong table. It is the offer that counts: the flexibility and choice. The fact that the company is providing options is recognizing that its people value different things. They like to relieve stress in different ways, connect and create in different ways, and celebrate in different ways. The options that are provided are not generation specific. They just recognize that different people like different things. Of course, this takes a lot of time and money, but if we understand that people have to come first in the future of work, this investment will cost pennies on the dollar compared to what the expenses would be of short tenure and a misaligned culture.

The Human Touch

The human touch counts. One of my favourite quotes comes from Benjamin Franklin: "Tell me and I forget. Teach me and I may remember. Involve me and I learn." Yet look at how we are training the next generation of employees. Instead of traditional face-to-face communication, we are telling them to watch a training video. Human contact is becoming less and less frequent, and the interactions between people are less meaningful and less personal.

Managing this next generation is going to require a major shift in the way many companies operate. Though it may seem counterintuitive, I believe we are going to have to manage people the old-fashioned way. In order to get the most out of people, we have to give them the time and attention needed to do the job well. No, this is not specific to the next generation because they need more, expect more, and are entitled to more. It is because the personal, human form of training works better, just as it did for their parents' generation.

● ● ●

Herein lies a major opportunity. The personal aspects of work differentiate jobs that require a similar skill set, and are incredibly important. By managing this generation through personal contact and interpersonal relationships, not by remotely observing or digitally guiding them, we deliberately create a tribe and community at work. Work will feel a lot less like work. And it will be done in a workplace to love.

8

Rethinking Work

*If we can make people's
lives better at work, we can
make people's lives better.*

For a job seeker, the real question is not what you want to do—it is how you want to do it, who you want to do it with, and why you want to do it. In other words, people need to think about the life they want to live. Then they can find a job that supports it.

Say, for example, I want to live on the water and spend as much time outside as possible. I love to golf and will do whatever it takes to avoid wearing a suit to work. I want to be able to connect with people and have conversations that are new and exciting every day. I want to work close to home and stay out of a big city. Now that I have understood the things that mean the most to me, and I know that I have the skills to be an accountant, it is very easy to filter out the industries and sectors that may not be a good fit and look for a job that fits the description of the things I want to do and the life I want to live. So, when I see a job posting come up for an accountant at my local golf course, I'm going to drive down there that day and tell them why I want to work for the course and how I'm going to be a great fit. *Then*, I'll follow up with a resumé so the employer knows that I have the skills and requirements to do the job.

Where the Next Generation Is Coming From

The next generation (whatever that is) coming into the workforce is in a terrible bind. We borrowed heavily to get that university or college degree, and we hoped—and our parents hoped—that the university education would land us one of the prime white-collar jobs that, at dinner tables across the country, our parents urged us to get. Instead, we found ourselves in fierce competition for that job— against other people our age. As we have seen, the number of students in Canadian universities has doubled while the population of the same age group has slipped three percent. In other words, there are more university graduates chasing the prime jobs.

Thousands of students are flooding top financial or consulting firms with applications for every choice job. While we try to beat the odds, many of us are living in our parents' homes. The number of Canadians in their twenties who are living in their parents' home has jumped from twenty-seven percent to forty-two percent since 1980.

Meanwhile, some industries—like forestry, mining, manufacturing, transportation, apparel, construction, and automotive—cannot find enough employees. It does not make sense, and I think the answer lies where the trouble began: at the family dinner table.

Parents often insist their children go to university. They mean well, of course, but they are not always considering the job that actually fits their children's wants and needs—and the lucrative, innovative, and purpose-driven careers that are out there.

Does this sound like the old-fashioned American Dream, the one that the Woodstock generation was supposed to reject? Most of them did not do that. Instead, they foisted the dream on their children—my generation.

You might think I am being a little ridiculous in generalizing parents' behaviours based on the number of young Canadians who have flooded into university. But it would appear that our parents' dream does not consider how we feel when our heads hit our pillows, or how excited we are on Monday morning about the coming week. It does not consider the strength of our families, or our feeling of satisfaction when we use our skills and talents to make a difference in the world we live in. Generally speaking, our parents consider what might drive the most dollars into our bank accounts. Not a bad concern to have, but we're looking to rethink work, and rethinking work isn't just about dollars and cents.

Parents may mean well, but when they pressure us to take jobs that are not connected with the things we care about, they are not helping us to be happy, fulfilled, and productive.

Rethinking Success

We need to shift not only how we articulate the values and experiences of the job but also how we talk about success.

• • •

The solution is a lot simpler than one might think.

Right now, too many people are chasing The Job, and then trying to build a life around it. It usually doesn't work. We might end up in the wrong city, working with people who are not our tribe. We work long hours, and we don't know why we're putting in so much effort. The high turnover rate of employees is ample evidence that something is wrong.

Here's a better way:

Redefining Success

Right now, society tells me that the most successful person is the one with the sexiest job title, most education, or greatest amount of accumulated finances or material goods. This needs to change. Instead of measuring success based on these traditional factors, I would suggest that we start measuring success based on happiness and fulfillment. If we compared smiles on our faces when we got home from work, perhaps there would be less conflict, less meaningless competition, and more support for each other.

Rethinking work, then, is bigger than just the work we have already discussed.

We have to start by figuring out what life we want to live. Then we can find a job that supports that life. This small change in perspective is crucial.

Every morning when we get up to brush our teeth and take a shower, we get a chance to look in the mirror and ask ourselves who we are, what we want to get out of the day, and what it is that makes us happy. Because we can continually revisit this and refine it, and constantly work on it, we can gain a better understanding of ourselves and of a potential job, or jobs, that we might occupy.

The opposite approach is where the risk lies. If you aim to be a highly paid management consultant, and you go to university with that goal, you might just get that job if you have a stellar academic track record. But how will you know if the life of a consultant, with its constant travel, often to less-than-appealing places, actually suits you?

In 2016, I had the honour of speaking to business and policy leaders from across the globe at the Milken Institute Global Conference. After the conference, I met with JuVan Langford, men's empowerment coach and founder of The Elevation Effect. He is an incredible individual, and during our conversation he asked me a powerful question: "Are you clear as to what it is you're running to?" When I stumbled over my words trying to find a response, he suggested that I was maybe already here. I told him that I had the ability to travel, grow, meet people, learn, be challenged, and discover on a daily basis. It was then that I realized that I had chosen a life that I wanted to live, and not a job. Success for me, in other words, wasn't about the money or the title; it was about freedom.

We all know the typical question we get during and after graduating from college: what do we want to do? We have been asked that question all our lives, and we may still not know the answer.

My suggestion, which may sound unorthodox, is: it doesn't matter what we do. That's right. It doesn't matter. The things we do at work are going to be largely the same: spending time on the phone, in meetings, and sending emails. What we talk and type about only matters in terms of how it makes us feel. What does matter is how we work, who we work with, and why we do what we do.

Let's get back to the college graduate who has her accounting degree and might not know where to go next. Perhaps it is not one of the big players that best fits her lifestyle. Perhaps the local golf course has an opening that would be perfect for her as she is nearly a professional golfer and loves to hit the links on the weekend and after work. Maybe then, a golf course would be the best fit for her.

Anyone in a corporate position likely fills a majority of the day talking on the phone, typing emails or reports, or attending some sort of meeting—regardless of the industry or company size. With that said, though, these actions do not matter as much as the feeling we get from them. If I am typing a message about my company, The DRYVER Group, knowing that if I land the deal or get my point across that someone may be able to live a happier life, then the feeling I get from what I do is going to keep me going. The "why" behind what I am doing is powerful enough to keep me engaged and connected to the work I am doing, not the action itself.

If we're rethinking work, let's rethink all jobs. Let's rethink the trades, for example. Take the job of a plumber. I bet there are not too many of us who were advised by our parents to be a plumber. Yet this job can be innovative, entrepreneurial, and creative. A plumber could have opportunities to manage a team and to work his own hours. He owns his own tools, and he certainly would be connected physically to the job. He can take pride in fixing a pressing problem for a client. There is no doubt he can see the difference his work makes: his success certainly makes someone's day a lot better. The job can be lucrative and allow a lifestyle focused around home, family, and friends.

Or take the classic job of an analyst or sales rep. The life she leads at work will depend on where she works. At a green-energy firm, she can say to herself that she's helping the world to be a cleaner, healthier place. Someone doing the numbers for a movie company may well enjoy the challenge of making a documentary or a movie come alive. Work for a small business that allows you to work wherever and whenever you want, as long as you get the job done on time, and you may appreciate the lifestyle that it allows you to live.

Again, it is not about what we do, but how we do it, who with, and why we do it.

• • •

We have to rethink what it means to be successful. We have to understand what it is we need to live a happy and fulfilling life. We have to understand what we value and what we have to do to achieve connection, ownership, and purpose in the work we do. We have to rethink work.

To accomplish this, no doubt there needs to be passion and drive to get the skills we need and to parlay that into a job. But in my view, you can acquire the skills for most jobs. Not long ago, I spent some time with a friend from high school. At that time, we all studied pretty much the same thing. But in just seven years, we had travelled in entirely different directions. She followed her deep passion to help other people. This led her to become a dental hygienist, and then to volunteer to travel to Guatemala to help those who are dealing with tooth decay from lack of dental hygiene and over-consumption of Coca-Cola. It was astonishing to see how the two of us had taken such different paths.

Thinking back on our conversation, I realized that we all can acquire almost any skill we need to put food on the table and a roof over our heads. All we really need is the drive to get there, and to feel connected when we arrive.

Conclusion

*We have an opportunity to
re-humanize the workplace and
turn the tables when it comes to
workplace satisfaction.*

We need to rethink work. We need to rethink it because people (especially those who are younger) are now quitting their jobs after being there less than three years. Careers aren't really careers anymore, they're short-term jobs. These departures are expensive and disruptive for companies and the people within them. It is no fun for people either when they drag their feet home and complain at the dinner table instead of enjoying their family life.

Why are so many people running for the door? We have the skills, to be sure, but the life at work does not make sense for us. Because work is bigger than just the task at hand; it is a true identifier of who we are. But this is not why we were recruited. We were recruited for our skills, but we are not feeling any connection to the mission of the company or its culture. We didn't see it coming. The company didn't tell the real story of what it was like to work there, and we didn't ask.

What is more, technology has turned offices into impersonal places. Training is done with videos. People do not talk with each other like we used to. The texting, typing, WhatsApping, Slacking, Facebooking, and Tweeting are all well and good in the name of speed and efficiency, but they strip life of emotion and expression, and that is a big trade-off.

People of all generations and ages need more. We need human contact, real conversation. At work, we need to be treated as human beings and not human "doings"—to riff off the Kurt Vonnegut quote.

What we need is what people used to have on the job: a boss who talks to us and gives us good feedback, a company with a mission that sounds like our own, co-workers we like and might even go out with for a beer or a hike after work. We need community and we need to belong.

We need to restore humanity in the workplace. We do not want to be treated as a stereotyped group of Millennials, Gen Xers, or, for that matter, any other generation. We want to be understood as whole individuals.

We will work better that way. In fact, everyone works better that way.

Does that sound expensive? Troublesome? Not worth the effort? Consider the alternative. The cost of turnover in a $75,000-per-year job is conservatively estimated at $15,000 each time a new person needs to be recruited and trained. Worse, though, is that I have heard horror stories of recruiting and training costing three or four times that, with tenure being eight to twelve months! People under thirty-five typically change jobs, at all salary levels, every three years. Consider how many jobs in your company are filled by people in this age group and do the math. (Someone once told me that if I thought hiring a great employee was expensive, the cost of hiring an average one would be much more. The difference was that I would pay the higher price for the average one later.)

But that is just the beginning.

For companies that rethink work, there is a significant upside. As we have seen, rethinking work does not mean changing what people do. It does mean rethinking how we work, who we work with, and why we work. It means talking about these things more than we do now. Actually, it just means talking more: meaningfully connecting more. If we can articulate this clearly for our employees and our prospective employees, we will have a workforce that wants to do the best for our mission. Employees won't just do the task because it is required; they will do it because they are connected to it and want to help make a larger impact. This will increase company productivity and improve performance. It will help to define corporate culture so that a company can be differentiated from its competitors, and can find the best prospects for its organization. After a while, if companies are successful at rethinking work, we will see a tipping point. Employees will be able to define the "people" part of the mission, vision, and values statements. In other words, they can tell prospective employees who they are and what it is like to work in the organization. That will be a more compelling image than any job posting with clichés about being a "team player" and "driven" could ever be. When people buy in to the real values of the workplace, they will create a community, a tribe, and they will feel that sense of belonging.

We are talking about culture. Whether we like it or not, each company has a culture. That culture, like energy, cannot be created or destroyed. It can change forms, though. It can be tweaked to ensure everybody is aligned, in terms of the character of the people, how they react to the created environment as well as how they work and for what purpose.

True, we cannot fix culture, but we can fix the way we classify people and talk about the offerings of a career. The first step is to stop using stereotypes to describe people—especially the young people known as Millennials. Instead, we should look at people based on the things they value and experiences they desire. Once we value each person for who he or she is and remove the falsely constructed assumption that they have the same qualities as the rest of a generation, we can focus on alignment, community, and connection between people and work.

This is a quick way to close the communication gap and the age gap between older people in the workplace and the next generation just entering it. It cannot just happen with a reply-all email, though. We need to do this face to face, in real conversation, and we even need to slow down. If we can depend less on technology and build meaningful relationships and friendships both inside and outside of work, there is no way we can't create a better place to work.

In the future, I believe people will go back to working in the office in order to feed that need for belonging. But the offices we return to won't be the offices our parents knew and despised back in the 1970s. Physical workplaces should be designed for the needs of the human beings who work there. Some individuals do their best work in a quiet space. Others work best on a kitchen table surrounded by people they can talk to. Workplaces of the future need to have both.

But more importantly, they need to be places where people have true work–life balance. Now that technology has blurred the line between work and outside-of-work life, work is taking on a different meaning for people my age, and for other people as well. It's not just a job. It's bigger than work. It's integrated into our lives.

This represents a big shift in the area of human resources. In the future, recruiting won't just be focused on the skills and requirements to do the job; it will be about the life at work, the culture of the workplace, and the alignment of people in the workplace. HR won't just be about mitigating people problems and dealing with payroll, benefits, and holidays; it will be about promotion of people and culture, and making sure a company's biggest assets are happy, advancing in their careers, and doing great work because they want to. As I have argued in this book, doing all that is needed to get the right people, who like the same things and the same experiences, is not a cost. It is a key investment in the organization's future, and it should be treated this way. The HR function in companies will be bigger than ever, because the ultimate puzzle to solve is people.

In rethinking work, we will find that we rethink the way we communicate work, and actually bring the job description to life. If we can bring people together based on who they are rather than which generation they are a part of or how old they are, we will respect and recognize people for the things they value. If we re-humanize the workplace, perhaps work will seem much less like work and much more like a community of people coming together to happily solve problems and move forward.

At the end of the day, work needs to be bigger than work. To make this happen, we need to rethink work for everyone.

References

About Careers. "How Often Do People Change Jobs," last
   modified June 14, 2016. http://jobsearch.about.com/
   od/employmentinformation/f/change-jobs.htm. (Last
   accessed on July 11, 2016)

Agrawal, Sanjeev. "How Companies Can Attract the Best
   College Talent," *Harvard Business Review*, March 17, 2014.
   https://hbr.org/2014/03/how-companies-can-attract-the-
   best-college-talent/. (Last accessed on July 11, 2016)

Bartleby.com, Inc. www.bartleby.com/73/195.html. (Last
   accessed on July 11, 2016)

Bench. "In a World Gone Mad, Bench Gives People Control
   over Their Financial Life," June 27, 2016, https://bench.co/
   careers/. (Last accessed on July 11, 2016)

Bercovici, Jeff. "Facebook is Getting More Popular – With Senior Citizens," *Forbes*, December 2013. www.forbes. com/sites/jeffbercovici/2013/12/30/facebook-is-getting-more-popular-with-senior-citizens/ #5b7d42b13cc6. (Last accessed on July 11, 2016)

Bersin. "Bersin and Associates' New Research Finds U.K. Talent Acquisition Spending Rose Six Percent in 2011," *Bersin by Deloitte*, December 2011. https://www.bersin.com/ News/Content.aspx?id=15071. (Last accessed on July 11, 2016)

Boushey, Heather, and Sarah Jane Glynn. "There Are Significant Business Costs to Replacing Employees," Center for American Progress, November 16, 2012. www.americanprogress.org/issues/labor/report/2012/ 11/16/44464/there-are-significant-business-costs-to-replacing-employees/. (Last accessed on July 11, 2016)

Bowden, Mark. "Tales of the Tyrant," *The Atlantic*, May 2002. www.theatlantic.com/magazine/archive/2002/05/tales-of-the-tyrant/302480/. (Last accessed on July 11, 2016)

Bureau of Labor Statistics. "Employee Tenure Summary," Economic News Release, last modified September 18, 2014. www.bls.gov/news.release/tenure.nr0.htm. (Last accessed on July 11, 2016)

Careers Advice. "Career Change Statistics: You Will Change Careers 7 Times in Your Life?" June 27, 2016.

www.careers-advice-online.com/career-change-statistics.
html. (Last accessed on July 11, 2016)

"Cloud Foundry Summit 2016," held at Santa Clara, CA,
May 22–26, 2016. https://cfsummit2016.sched.org/
event/6aVk/keynote-technology-and-the-threat-of-a-
jobless-future-martin-ford-author-of-rise-of-the-robots.
(Last accessed on July 11, 2016)

CrossFit Fortis. http://crossfitfortis.ca/crossfit/what-is-
crossfit/. (Last accessed July 11, 2016)

Cubiks. "Cubiks International Survey on Job and
Cultural Fit." July 2016. http://admin.cubiks.com/
SiteCollectionDocuments/Files%20ENG/Research%20
Studies%20ENG/Cubiks%20Survey%20Results%20
July%202013.pdf. (Last accessed on July 11, 2016)

Dobby, Christine. "Telus Pays the Price for Swapping CEOs",
The Globe and Mail, April 2016. www.theglobeandmail.
com/report-on-business/telus-pays-co-ceos-a-total-of-
241-million-in-2015/article29516536/. (Last accessed on
July 11, 2016)

Evans, Dave. "The Internet of Things: How the Next Evolu-
tion of the Internet Is Changing Everything," Cisco Internet Business Solutions Group, July 2011. www.cisco.com/
c/dam/en_us/about/ac79/docs/innov/IoT_IBSG_
0411FINAL.pdf. (Last accessed July 11, 2016)

Fortune. "100 Best Companies to Work For, 2016," June 27, 2016. http://fortune.com/best-companies/. (Last accessed on July 11, 2016)

Gordon, Stephen. "Trends in Job Tenure," Worthwhile Canadian Initiative, January 4, 2011. http://worthwhile. typepad.com/worthwhile_canadian_initi/2011/01/ trends-in-job-tenure.html. (Last accessed on July 11, 2016)

Gellman, Lindsay. "Millennials: Love Them or Let Them Go," *Wall Street Journal*, last modified May 6, 2015. www.wsj.com/articles/how-employers-wrangle-restless-millennials-1430818203. (Last accessed on July 11, 2016)

Goudreau, Jenna. "Do You Suffer From Workplace Anxiety?", *Forbes*, February 2011. www.forbes.com/sites/ jennagoudreau/2011/02/08/do-you-suffer-from-workplace-anxiety-worry-stress-fear-office-most-common/#3cfbb85937f3. (Last accessed on July 11, 2016)

Huang, Daniel and Lindsay Gellman. "Millennial Employees Confound Big Banks," *Wall Street Journal*, April 2016. www.wsj.com/articles/millennial-employees-confound-big-banks-1460126369. (Last accessed on July 11, 2016)

"Living Arrangements of Young Adults Aged 20 to 29," *Statistics Canada*, December 2015. www12.statcan.gc.ca/ census-recensement/2011/as-sa/98-312-x/98-312-x2011003_3-eng.cfm. (Last accessed on July 11, 2016)

Lorsch, Jay W., and McTague, Emily. "Culture Is Not the Culprit," *Harvard Business Review*, April 2016. https://hbr.org/

2016/04/culture-is-not-the-culprit. (Last accessed on
July 11, 2016)

Manjoo, Farhad. "The Happiness Machine: How Google
Became Such a Great Place to Work," *Slate*, January 2013.
www.slate.com/articles/technology/technology/2013/
01/google_people_operations_the_secrets_of_the_world_
s_most_scientific_human.html. (Last accessed on July 11,
2016)

Manjoo, Farhad. "Corporate America Chases the Mythical
Millennial," *New York Times*, May 2016. www.nytimes.com/
2016/05/26/technology/corporate-america-chases-the-
mythical-millennial.html. (Last accessed on July 11, 2016)

McGregor, Jenna. "What the Most Productive Workers
Have in Common," *Washington Post*, August 2014.
www.washingtonpost.com/news/on-leadership/wp/
2014/08/05/what-the-most-productive-workers-have-in-
common/. (Last accessed on July 11, 2016)

Meister, Jeanne. "Job Hopping Is the 'New Normal' for Millennials: Three Ways to Prevent a Human Resource Night-
mare," Forbes Leadership, last modified August 14, 2012.
www.forbes.com/sites/jeannemeister/2012/08/14/job-
hopping-is-the-new-normal-for-millennials-three-ways-
to-prevent-a-human-resource-nightmare/#55446a195508.
(Last accessed on July 11, 2016)

Merhar, Christina. "Employee Retention: The Real Cost
of Losing an Employee," Zane Benefits, February 4,
2016. www.zanebenefits.com/blog/bid/312123/

Employee-Retention-The-Real-Cost-of-Losing-an-Employee. (Last accessed on July 11, 2016)

Millar, Erin and Ilona Dougherty. "Beyond Rehearsal for the Real World," *The Globe and Mail*, October 2015. www.theglobeandmail.com/news/national/education/canadian-university-report/beyond-rehearsal-for-the-real-world/article26898209/. (Last accessed on July 11, 2016)

"Millennials and Financial Literacy – The Struggle with Personal Finance," *PWC*, 2015. www.pwc.com/us/en/about-us/corporate-responsibility/assets/pwc-millennials-and-financial-literacy.pdf. (Last accessed on July 11, 2016)

"Millennials in Adulthood," *Pew Research Center*, March 2014. www.pewsocialtrends.org/2014/03/07/millennials-in-adulthood/. (Last accessed on July 11, 2016)

Milken Institute. "Jobs and Technology: Is Any Job Safe?" May 3, 2016. www.youtube.com/watch?v=OQ7ul23_Ydw. (Last accessed on July 11, 2016)

Monster Worldwide Inc. http://jobview.monster.ca/retail-stock-shipper-square-one-job-mississauga-on-ca-16580 6359.aspx. (Last accessed on July 11, 2016)

Net Impact. "Talent Report: What Workers Want in 2012," *Net Impact*, May 2012. https://netimpact.org/sites/default/files/documents/what-workers-want-2012.pdf. (Last accessed on July 11, 2016)

Phelps, Stan. "Google Averages 130 Applicants to Make One Hire," *Smart Recruiters*, August 2014. www.smartrecruiters. com/blog/google-averages-130-applicants-to-make-one-hire/. (Last accessed on July 11, 2016)

Rezvani, Selena. "Five Trends Driving Workplace Diversity in 2015," *Forbes*, February 2015. www.forbes.com/sites/work-in-progress/2015/02/03/20768/#4851939c34c9. (Last accessed on July 11, 2016)

Rieger, Sarah. "Fort McMurray Fire: Suncor Pilot Broke Rules to Fly Pets to Safety," *Huffington Post*, May 2016. www.huffingtonpost.ca/2016/05/12/fort-mcmurray-pets_n_9936426.html. (Last accessed on July 11, 2016)

Rivera, Lauren A. Guess Who Doesn't Fit In at Work," *New York Times*, May 2015. www.nytimes.com/2015/05/31/opinion/sunday/guess-who-doesnt-fit-in-at-work.html?_r=4. (Last accessed on July 11, 2016)

Singh, Jasky. "Get Sh*t Done – One Hashtag That'll 10x Your Output… It Did for Me," *beyourself*, November 2015. https://byrslf.co/get-sh-t-done-one-hashtag-that-ll-10x-your-output-it-did-for-me-3d3923527960#.emi1d779u. (Last accessed on July 11, 2016)

Soydanbay. "Why do Mission Statements Suck," *Soydanbay*, August 2010. https://soydanbay.com/2010/08/09/why-do-mission-statements-suck/#more-442. (Last accessed on July 11, 2016)

Sullivan, Dr. John. "Hiring Job Hoppers: 10 Reasons Why They Are So Very Valuable," Ere Media, last modified June 2, 2015. www.eremedia.com/tlnt/hiring-job-hoppers-10-reasons-why-they-are-so-very-valuable/. (Last accessed on July 11, 2016)

Vonnegut, Kurt. Goodreads. www.goodreads.com/quotes/817241-i-am-a-human-being-not-a-human-doing. (Last accessed July 11, 2016)

Weber, Lauren. "Your Resume vs. Oblivion," *Wall Street Journal*, January 2012. www.wsj.com/articles/SB1000142 405297020462420457717894103494130. (Last accessed on July 11, 2016)

"Workplace Stress," *The American Institute of Stress* www.stress.org/workplace-stress/. (Last accessed on July 11, 2016)

About the Author

Eric Termuende grew up in Cranbrook, B.C., Canada, with his parents, Tim and Joyce, and his younger brother, Joel. Eric graduated from Haskayne School of Business at the University of Calgary in 2014. He was vice-president operations and finance for the Students Union and was chosen as class ambassador for his graduating class. He went on to co-found Gen Y Inc. (now The DRYVER Group), which led to public speaking engagements and to working across the country and internationally. In 2015, Eric was recognized by American Express as a Top 100 Emerging Innovator Under 35 Globally and was elected to sit on the Leadership Committee for the Canadian G20 YEA. Shortly after, Eric signed with the National Speakers Bureau and, only ten months later, was selected by his agency as one of the top speakers in Canada. Currently, Eric and his team are focussed on building DRYVER and sharing the importance of the messages in this book through the work they do and the appearances they make on stages across the world. Eric lives in Vancouver and spends his spare time on the city's seawall and hiking the many trails of the West Coast.